FLUID CONNECTIONS

Celebrating the Niagara River's Journey
from Lake-to-Lake

Writing by Mark Donnelly, PhD.
Photography by Mark Donnelly & Friends

RPSS Publishing • Buffalo, New York
www.rpsspublishing.com

From the grain elevators of Buffalo,

to the mist of the Falls

and the vineyards of Niagara-on-the-Lake,

the Niagara River has carried war and peace,

power and spectacle, industry and imagination.

This is the story of a short river

with a long legacy,

and a current that connects nations,

communities, and centuries.

Hardcover: ISBN: 978-1-956688-56-6   Perfect Bound: ISBN: 978-1-956688-57-3

First Edition - Printed in the United States of America
www.rpsspublishing.com

Flow

On the Cover: Each Wednesday evening, sails fill the Buffalo Harbor for spirited races, blending competition, camaraderie, and stunning Lake Erie sunsets along the city's waterfront.

Opposite: The Lower River from the shore of Devil's Hole

The River ~~River~~ *Strait* Between Two Lakes

The Niagara River is one of the shortest rivers in the world, yet one of the most storied. In just thirty-six miles it rushes from Lake Erie to Lake Ontario, carving out a path that has shaped nations, industries, and imaginations. For centuries it has served as a natural boundary, a highway of commerce, a source of immense power, and, perhaps most famously, a stage for wonder and spectacle.

This book follows the Niagara River on its journey, tracing the water's course bend by bend, town by town. It is a river that is never still. At its head, in Buffalo, New York, the river surges out of Lake Erie beneath the Peace Bridge, linking the United States with Canada at Fort Erie, Ontario. From there it winds past bustling cities and quiet hamlets, across rapids and around islands, until it thunders over the edge at Niagara Falls–the most famous cataract on earth. Downstream, the river narrows through a wild gorge, swirling into whirlpools and racing through rapids before it calms again, broadening into fertile farmland and vineyard country, and finally emptying into Lake Ontario beneath the shadow of Old Fort Niagara.

The Niagara is more than geography; it is also history. Indigenous peoples lived along its banks for centuries, weaving stories of spirit and power into its waters. European settlers fought wars for it, engineers tamed it, daredevils risked their lives to challenge it, and millions of visitors from around the world continue to marvel at it. The river powered the rise of Buffalo's grain elevators, North Tonawanda's lumber mills, and the hydroelectric stations that lit entire cities. It also inspired parks and preserves, a conservation movement, and one of the earliest international efforts to share a natural wonder.

Entertainment and spectacle have always coursed alongside the Niagara's waters. The roar of the Falls became the backdrop for weddings, honeymoons, and holiday excursions. Tents and taverns gave way to grand hotels, casinos, and amusement districts. Tightrope walkers balanced above its depths, barrel-riders tested its plunge, and today, boat tours and observation decks bring millions closer to the spray each year.

Yet for all its fame, the Niagara River is also a collection of quieter places– of fishing docks and ferry crossings, of riverfront neighborhoods and family festivals. Each community along its banks, from Buffalo and Tonawanda to Lewiston and Niagara-on-the-Lake, tells a piece of the larger story.

To follow the Niagara River is to follow a current of history, culture, and natural power unlike any other. It is a river that connects lakes, countries, and people. In the chapters ahead, we will journey along its length–from Lake Erie to Lake Ontario–stopping at the towns, islands, and landmarks that give this short but mighty river its enduring place in the world's imagination.

A Landscape Written in Water and Stone

The Great Lakes and the Niagara River are a dialogue between the very old and the very new. They rest on billion-year-old rifts and Paleozoic reefs, yet their present forms are largely the work of ice that vanished only yesterday in geologic time. Niagara Falls itself is a teenager among landscapes, still reshaping its gorge as we watch.

For the visitor, the beauty is immediate: a horizon-wide lake, a roaring cataract, a dizzying whirlpool. For the geologist, the wonder lies in the script beneath: a tale of rifting, seas, glaciers, and rivers, written in stone and carried forward by water. To stand at Niagara is to stand on a page that is still being written.

THE LONG VIEW: FROM RIFT TO RIM

The Great Lakes and the Niagara River look timeless, but they are anything but. Their story begins over a billion years ago with the Midcontinent Rift, a vast wound in North America's crust that almost split the continent in two. Around Lake Superior, lava poured out in titanic floods, cooling into basalt that still anchors the basin's depth. Though the rift failed, the crust sagged and stayed weak—a structural low that later ice sheets and water would deepen into the world's largest freshwater system.

By the Paleozoic era, shallow seas had crept across this part of the continent. Layer upon layer of limestone, dolostone, sandstone, and shale piled up, building the foundations of Michigan, Ontario, and western New York. The Niagara Escarpment—today the ledge over which the river plunges—formed not from earthquakes or faults but from the stubborn endurance of Silurian dolostone resting atop weaker shale.

Nature's architecture was set: a hard roof, a soft floor. All that remained was for time, ice, and water to carve drama into the landscape.

ICE AS SCULPTOR

The Pleistocene was the age of ice. The Laurentide Ice Sheet pressed across the Midwest and Northeast, more than a mile thick in places. It gouged out the Great Lakes basins, deepened valleys, and bulldozed soft bedrock. As the ice advanced and retreated, it left behind moraines, drumlins, and the great over-deepenings that now cradle inland seas.

When the ice finally began to retreat around 20,000 years ago, meltwater pooled in every depression. These waters became temporary proglacial lakes, rising and falling as outlets opened and closed. Beaches formed far above today's shorelines, ghostly reminders of vanished lakes like Algonquin, Whittlesey, and Iroquois.

Opposite: The rapids below the Falls just about to enter the Whirlpool

LAKE IROQUOIS'S ANCIENT BEACH

Around 13,000–14,000 years ago, the Ontario basin held a vast proglacial water body: Glacial Lake Iroquois. With the St. Lawrence outlet still dammed by ice, the lake stood about 30 meters higher than modern Lake Ontario. Its waters spread wide across southern Ontario and New York, leaving a telltale ridge–the Iroquois Beach–that can still be traced today.

Stand in Toronto, and you may find yourself walking along a sandy rise now lined with houses and streets, unaware that it was once a shoreline where waves lapped against an icy horizon. The beach's present tilt, rising dramatically toward Kingston, is the fingerprint of isostatic rebound: the crust springing back after the crushing weight of ice. In a sense, Lake Iroquois still haunts the landscape.

BIRTH OF A RIVER

As the glaciers melted, Lake Erie sought an escape. Water spilled over the Niagara Escarpment near modern Lewiston–Queenston, carving the first Niagara Falls. At first, the cataract stood where the escarpment drops off; then, as water undercut the shale beneath the dolostone cap, the brink collapsed in blocks, retreating upstream. Over 12,000 years, the falls have carved a gorge seven miles long, inching steadily toward Lake Erie.

The river's route, however, was not entirely new. Pre-glacial rivers had cut valleys across the escarpment, only to be buried by ice and sediment. One of these, the St. David's Buried Gorge, would later be reawakened in spectacular fashion.

THE WHIRLPOOL'S HIDDEN PAST

About 4,000 years ago, Niagara Falls retreated into the buried valley of St. David's Gorge. Unlike solid dolostone, this valley was clogged with glacial sands and gravels–soft material that water devoured quickly. The river captured the gorge, hollowed out its fill, and created the violent bend and deep pool we now call the Niagara Whirlpool.

Today, the whirlpool is one of the most dramatic features of the river, a swirling gyre of green water hemmed in by cliffs. Yet it owes its existence to an older river, long vanished, whose valley became a shortcut for Niagara's relentless erosion. In a sense, the Whirlpool is a geological memory come alive.

Above: Formed by the retreat of Niagara Falls, the Niagara Whirlpool swirls with powerful currents offering visitors a breathtaking glimpse of nature's raw force and geologic history.

WATERFALL IN MOTION

The mechanism of Niagara's retreat is simple but powerful. The Lockport Dolostone at the crest resists erosion, while the underlying shale erodes easily. Water crashes against the base, spray and frost loosen rock, and eventually, the overhanging dolostone breaks off in massive slabs. The process repeats, year after year, century after century.

Before human intervention, the falls moved upstream at three to five feet a year. Since the mid-20th century, when flow was regulated for hydropower and scenic preservation, retreat has slowed to roughly a foot per year. Even so, Niagara continues its march toward Lake Erie. In another 15,000 years, if left alone, the falls may cut back into the lake itself.

THE HOLOCENE LAKES

While Niagara gnawed into the escarpment, the Great Lakes themselves stabilized. The Nipissing phase raised water levels around 5,000 years ago, flooding lowlands and knitting Michigan, Huron, and Superior into a vast inland sea. By about 3,000 years ago, levels approached modern conditions. On Lake Erie, spits like Long Point began to grow, shaped by waves and currents into delicate sandscapes.

But the lakes are not static. The crust continues to rebound, rising faster in the north than in the south, slowly tilting basins and altering outlets. Climate change drives shorter-term fluctuations: lake levels rise and fall in cycles that still frustrate shoreline dwellers and delight geologists.

Right: A view from beneath the American Falls

11

WATSON
ELEVATOR

12

The Makers of Buffalo
A Story in Six Lives

Buffalo's birth was not the work of chance, nor of any one man.
It was the sum of visions: Ellicott's geometry, Wilkeson's harbor, Clinton's canal,
Hawley's pen, Porter's rivalry, Chapin's guardianship.
Each brought something indispensable.
Together, they transformed a frontier hamlet into the Queen City of the Lakes.

Today, the city still bears their imprint. Niagara Square radiates Ellicott's plan. The harbor Wilkeson built remains the heart of the waterfront. Clinton's canal lies quiet, its glory past, yet its path shaped the region. Hawley's dream reminds us that ideas can be born in obscurity. Porter's lost cause at Black Rock is remembered in neighborhood names. Chapin's resilience lives on in Buffalo's stubborn pride.

Six men, six lives, and one city, born from their labors, their rivalries, and their belief that even a windswept marsh at the edge of Lake Erie could become something great

.A Frontier Waiting for Its Fate

At the turn of the nineteenth century, western New York was a wilderness of promise. The forests pressed thick to the shores of Lake Erie, broken only by Native trails and a few fragile clearings where white settlers had pitched their cabins. Buffalo was not yet Buffalo, but a modest hamlet on the edge of marshland, with more geese than people and more doubts than prospects.

And yet, within half a century, this place would become the "Queen City of the Lakes," the terminus of the Erie Canal, a booming port through which flowed the grain and goods of the interior. How did such a transformation occur? Not by accident, but by the stubborn visions of men who, in different ways, refused to let Buffalo die in obscurity.

This is their story – told through six lives: Joseph Ellicott, Samuel Wilkeson, DeWitt Clinton, Jesse Hawley, Peter Porter, and Cyrenius Chapin. Each played a part in Buffalo's birth, whether by pen or plow, by compass or cannon, by law, politics, or sheer grit. Together, their efforts form not just biography but a collective epic: the making of Buffalo.

Opposite: An illustration of the early days of Buffalo's busy harbor.

JOSEPH ELLICOTT – THE SURVEYOR'S DREAM

Joseph Ellicott (1760–1826) was one of the most forceful and visionary figures in the early settlement of Western New York. A man of restless energy, he imposed order and ambition upon a raw frontier and left an imprint still visible today.

MASTER SURVEYOR AND TOWN BUILDER

In 1797, as chief surveyor for the Holland Land Company, Ellicott laid out the boundaries of millions of acres of Western New York. His most enduring plan was for Buffalo, where he designed a radial street pattern inspired by Pierre L'Enfant's Washington, D.C. Ellicott placed mill sites, town centers, and transportation routes precisely as he envisioned them, carving communities out of wilderness with his will and authority.

He became not just a land agent but a judge for Genesee County, a civic leader who blended technical skill with a hard-nosed sense of control. Settlers relied on him to chart their world, and he delivered, sometimes brusquely, always decisively. He has been described as short-tempered and tactless; indeed, he did not suffer fools gladly. He was, however, a generous agent, supporting poor landless families with liberal credit, offering free land to support inns along new roads, and donating money and land for churches and schools.

THE ERIE CANAL VISIONARY

Ellicott was also among the first to advocate for a grand canal linking the Hudson River to Lake Erie. Appointed as the very first Erie Canal Commissioner, he helped set in motion the project that would transform New York State into the Empire State. He lived long enough to see construction begin in 1821 and to celebrate its completion in 1825, vindicating his vision.

DECLINE AND TRAGEDY

For all his achievements, Ellicott's final years were clouded by deteriorating mental health, with symptoms resembling schizophrenia. Plagued by paranoia and deepening instability, he was admitted by family and friends to an asylum in New York City. In 1826, despair overcame him and he ended his life by hanging.

LEGACY

Ellicott's legacy is one of vision: a brilliant planner and canal pioneer whose force of will shaped Western New York.

A 1828 map of Buffalo

An early look at Buffalo Harbor

SAMUEL WILKESON - THE HARBOR BUILDER

After Buffalo was burned to the ground in December 1813, few thought it could rise again. Families fled barefoot through the snow as British troops and their Native allies set fire to homes, barns, and shops. In the morning, only chimneys stood. Rival Black Rock, just upriver, looked the better bet for survival.

But among the ashes walked Samuel Wilkeson, a Pennsylvania-born frontiersman turned judge, merchant, and civic leader. Wilkeson believed Buffalo could be more than a smoldering ruin. He believed it could be a harbor city – if only it had a harbor.

Lake Erie was cruel to Buffalo's shallow shoreline. Sandbars clogged the creek, storms wrecked vessels, and skeptics scoffed at the notion that this marsh could host ships. Black Rock, with its sheltered riverfront, seemed the obvious choice for the Erie Canal's western terminus.

Wilkeson disagreed. With no engineering degree, only observation and audacity, he proposed building piers to guide the current and scour a channel. In 1820 he put his own money and muscle to the task, rallying townsmen to drive piles and dredge. He worked in mud up to his knees, leading by example.

Against odds, the harbor took form. State commissioners, once skeptical, were impressed. When the Erie Canal opened in 1825, Buffalo had a working port. Grain and lumber poured in, warehouses rose, the population boomed. Buffalo, not Black Rock, became the canal city.

As mayor in 1836, Wilkeson guided Buffalo through its growing pains. He embodied the town's resilience: a man who took a burned-out village and willed it into a city. If Ellicott gave Buffalo its skeleton, Wilkeson gave it its beating heart – a harbor that made commerce flow.

DeWitt Clinton – Statesman of Destiny

While Wilkeson wrestled with piers and sandbars, DeWitt Clinton was wrestling with politics. A towering figure in New York public life – Mayor of New York City, U.S. Senator, Governor – Clinton was ambitious, imperious, and visionary.

His great cause was the Erie Canal. When first proposed, it was mocked as folly: "Clinton's Ditch," critics jeered. How could one state cut a 363-mile waterway through forest and swamp? Who would pay for it? Why not leave such dreams to muskrats and frogs?

Clinton pressed on. He argued that the canal would bind the Atlantic coast to the Great Lakes, turn New York into the Empire State, and make its farmers and merchants rich. He carried the legislature, raised funds, and drove the project forward.

For Buffalo, Clinton's canal was everything. The debate over its western terminus – Buffalo or Black Rock – was fierce. Clinton listened to both sides, but Wilkeson's harbor work and Ellicott's city plan tipped the balance. Buffalo won.

When the canal opened in 1825, Clinton rode in the lead boat from Buffalo to Albany, carrying a keg of Lake Erie water. At New York Harbor, he poured it into the Atlantic – the "wedding of the waters." Cannons roared, bells rang, celebrations spread from Manhattan to the frontier.

Buffalo's destiny was sealed. Clinton, though no Buffalonian, had made it the gateway to the West.

Jesse Hawley– The Prisoner Who Dreamed

Decades before Clinton's triumph, in a debtors' prison in Canandaigua, a failed flour merchant named Jesse Hawley had dreamed it all.

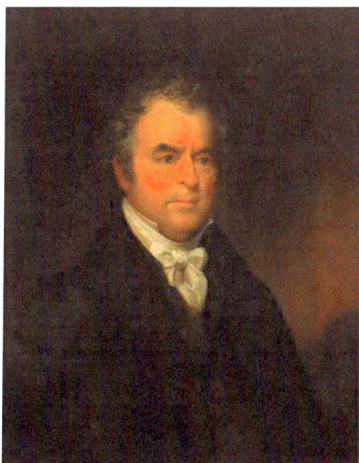

Hawley's grievance was simple: it cost too much to move wheat. Roads were rutted, wagons slow, rivers unreliable. He imagined a canal across New York, carrying flour from the Genesee country to market in New York City.

In 1807–08, under the pen name "Hercules," Hawley published fourteen essays in the Genesee Messenger. He described a canal 363 miles long, 40 feet wide, 4 feet deep, with locks, costs, and tolls calculated. He wrote from a cell, without maps or resources, yet his vision proved uncannily accurate.

At first, he was mocked. But Clinton and others later drew upon his work. In effect, the Erie Canal was born in Hawley's prison papers.

Hawley never grew rich or powerful. He lived to see the canal open, but not as its celebrated father. Yet Buffalo owed him much. Without his pen, there might have been no canal; without the canal, no harbor city. Hawley was Buffalo's unseen benefactor, its future written in ink behind bars.

Peter Buell Porter – The Necessary Rival

If Wilkeson was Buffalo's builder, Peter Buell Porter was its rival. Yale-educated, a general in the War of 1812, congressman, and landowner, Porter was Black Rock's champion.

Black Rock had the natural harbor Buffalo lacked. Porter invested heavily, built docks and mills, and lobbied furiously for it to be the canal's terminus. His arguments were sound, his influence immense. For a time, it seemed Buffalo might lose.

But Wilkeson's harbor project swung momentum. The state chose Buffalo. Black Rock withered, annexed into Buffalo in 1853. Porter lost the battle, but his rivalry forced Buffalo to fight harder, to innovate, to prove itself.

Porter went on to serve as Secretary of War under President John Quincy Adams. His national reputation survived, even if his dream for Black Rock did not.

In Buffalo's victory, Porter was the necessary antagonist. His challenge sharpened Buffalo's resolve. Without his pressure, Wilkeson's harbor might never have been built.

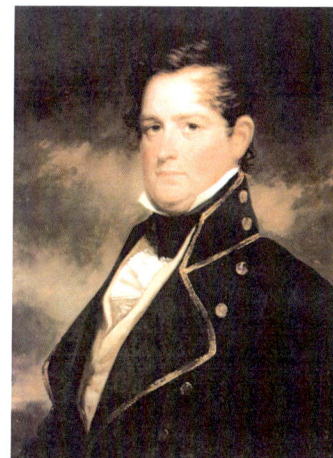

DR. CYRENIUS CHAPIN AND THE WAR OF 1812

The War of 1812 was fought not only by armies but by towns and communities straddling the Niagara frontier. Few figures embodied this struggle more vividly than Dr. Cyrenius Chapin of Buffalo. A physician by training and a militia officer by necessity, Chapin blurred the line between healer and warrior, civic leader and rogue. He was also a proud Freemason, a rare Federalist who broke with his party to support the war, and a man infamous for his fondness for strong drink, colorful profanity, and reckless daring.

A FRONTIER DOCTOR TURNED RAIDER

Born in 1769, Chapin practiced medicine in Buffalo for a decade before deciding that war offered more thrills than the sickroom. At 44, he took command of the mounted volunteers recruited at Buffalo. Their raids across the Niagara River were bold, destructive, and often lucrative, earning them the nickname "the Forty Thieves." For Chapin, the war was both patriotic duty and personal adventure.

QUEENSTON HEIGHTS

Chapin first made his mark at Queenston Heights in October 1812, when most militia refused to cross into Canada. He not only crossed but fought fiercely before being captured. Exchanged soon after, he returned to Buffalo with a reputation for audacity.

BEAVER DAMS: CAPTOR BECOMES CAPTOR

In June 1813, Chapin and 28 of his men were captured during the Battle of Beaver Dams. Escorted toward Kingston by boat under a guard of 16 British soldiers, Chapin bided his time. When the guards stopped to drink grog, he struck. The Americans overpowered them, seized the vessel, and forced their astonished captors into captivity.

There was, however, one problem: Chapin didn't know how to sail. His triumphant return turned slapstick when he ran the captured boat hard onto the rocks near Fort George. Chapin marched in, his own captors now his prisoners.

THE BURNING OF BUFFALO

On December 30, 1813, British regulars and their Native allies descended on Buffalo. Chapin rallied defenders with what little they had, including a decrepit cannon barrel strapped to a wagon. It managed one blast before collapsing in pieces. Outnumbered and outgunned, the defense crumbled, but their resistance delayed the British long enough for hundreds of civilians to escape.

As the militia broke and ran, Chapin gave his famous shout:
"Every man for himself & the Devil for us all!"

The British torched Buffalo, reducing it to ashes. He tended to the wounded, comforted survivors, and urged the town to rebuild.

CAPTIVITY AND RETURN

Chapin's reckless courage came at a price. Captured again in 1814, he was transported to Montreal, where he remained imprisoned until his release in September. Returning to Buffalo, he found his home in ruins but his spirit unbroken.

LEGACY

After the war, Chapin rebuilt his medical office and house on its original foundation. He resumed practicing medicine, helped establish the Erie County Medical Society, and promoted agriculture through the local farming society. He died in 1838, remembered as Buffalo's "warrior-doctor"–the man who stood when standing seemed impossible.

Opposite: During the Burning of Buffalo in December 1813, Dr. Cyrenius Chapin, physician turned militia leader, stood with townspeople and a lone cannon strapped to an old wagon to resist the advancing British, embodying the frontier community's courage in its darkest hour.

Lake Erie's Outlet

The story of the Niagara River begins where Lake Erie lets go. At the river's head, the waters of one of North America's Great Lakes funnel into a narrow channel that quickly becomes a current. Here, at Buffalo, New York, on the American side, and Fort Erie, Ontario, on the Canadian shore, the Niagara is born.

It is a peculiar beginning. Unlike many rivers, the Niagara is not a mountain stream carving its way toward the sea. It is the link in a chain, the natural outlet of one Great Lake draining into another. Its waters have already traveled far–from the farthest reaches of Minnesota and Michigan, down through Lake Superior, Lake Huron, and Lake Erie– before tumbling into this short but powerful passage. What makes the Niagara unique is not its length but its intensity: every drop of water in all four of those lakes will eventually thunder over Niagara Falls. When the young United States looked westward in the early 19th century, Buffalo was still a sleepy village. The turning point came with the completion of the Erie Canal in 1825. Suddenly, Buffalo became the hinge between canal traffic and the Great Lakes, and the Niagara River was the watery road leading out to the continent's heart. Grain elevators rose like cathedrals along the riverfront, their machinery powered by the wind, steam, and eventually electricity harnessed from the Falls downstream.

Buffalo's relationship to the Niagara was both practical and cultural. Steamboats, barges, and freighters crowded its waterfront, carrying goods east and west. Immigrants poured through its docks, making the city one of the great melting pots of the 19th century. The river gave Buffalo its industry, its prosperity, and eventually its moniker: "Queen City of the Lakes."

Opposite: The tall ship "The Spirit of Buffalo" exiting the Buffalo River | Above: City of Buffalo skyline.

ERIE CANAL

The advent of the Erie Canal arguably made Buffalo the center of the known universe. It was the crossroads connecting the manufactured products from the east with the rich agricultural bounty of the west. The building of the Erie Canal became the principal driver behind Buffalo's explosive growth in the mid-to-late 19th and early 20th centuries.

In 1825, Buffalo became was the focus of the most demanding engineering projects in the country. Built between 1817 and 1825, the original Erie Canal traversed 363 miles from Albany to Buffalo. Originally four feet deep and 40 feet wide, with removed soil piled on the downhill side to form a walkway known as a towpath. It cut through fields, forests, rocky cliffs, and swamps; crossed rivers on aqueducts; and overcame hills with 83 lift locks. Although its builders borrowed and adapted ideas and techniques from earlier European canals, they applied them with audacity on an unprecedented scale.

Despite the Canal Terminus's lofty role during its 1860s heyday, the waterfront was the polar opposite of paradise. It was chock full of riots and fun, emancipation and war, booze, brothels, battles, and more, depicting a wild and wondrously wicked, absolutely ruddy hell of a place to romp and hope to survive.

Left: Governor Dewitt Clinton on the inaugural trip on the Erie Canal aboard the Seneca.

Opposite: Along the Erie Canal, steady-footed mules once walked the towpaths, pulling heavily laden canalboats. Perhaps, one was named Sal.

Grain Elevators: Castles of Industry

Perhaps nothing defines Buffalo's riverfront legacy more than its grain elevators. Before their invention, unloading grain was a slow, backbreaking process done by hand. In 1842, Joseph Dart and engineer Robert Dunbar revolutionized the trade by building the world's first steam-powered grain elevator on the Buffalo River, a tributary of the Niagara. Using conveyor belts and buckets, the machine could scoop grain from a ship's hold and pour it into storage bins in minutes rather than days.

The idea spread rapidly, and soon Buffalo's skyline bristled with towering elevators—some of them vast concrete silos rising like modernist cathedrals. The city became the largest grain transfer hub in the world. At their peak, more than fifty elevators lined the riverfront, able to handle millions of bushels of wheat flowing from the Midwest to markets in the East and Europe.

Architects took notice. The stark, functional forms of Buffalo's elevators inspired European modernists like Walter Gropius and Le Corbusier, who saw in them a purity of design—a kind of accidental poetry in concrete. Buffalo, in turn, became not only an industrial giant but an architectural muse, its riverfront structures influencing modern architecture across the globe.

A WATERFRONT OF WORK AND WONDER

The riverfront was not merely functional—it was monumental. Elevators such as the Concrete-Central Elevator and the Marine A were massive enough to awe even hardened dockworkers. Bridges leapt across channels, their steel trusses rising against the horizon. Rail yards, warehouses, and shipyards created an industrial landscape that blended engineering with

Right: At Buffalo's bustling grain elevators, Scoopers, tough laborers who unloaded grain by hand, paused from their grueling work to rest, capturing a rare moment of camaraderie amid one of the city's hardest and most storied jobs.

artistry, even if its beauty was unintended.

For those who lived in Buffalo, the riverfront was part of daily life. The air smelled of grain dust, the whistle of tugboats echoed at dawn, and the clang of iron rails and machinery filled the day. To immigrants who labored there, the waterfront represented opportunity, however hard-earned. To visiting architects and writers, it was a vision of the future—an urban landscape built not for show but for sheer necessity, and all the more striking for it.

DECLINE AND ABANDONMENT

By the mid-20th century, Buffalo's grain trade declined as new shipping routes through the St. Lawrence Seaway bypassed the city. Factories closed, docks fell silent, and the once-bustling canal basin was filled in and paved over. The waterfront that had birthed Buffalo's greatness became a graveyard of rusting machinery and empty lots. For decades, Buffalo turned its back on the river, and the once-proud grain elevators stood like forgotten monuments.

DECLINE AND ABANDONMENT

By the mid-20th century, Buffalo's grain trade declined as new shipping routes through the St. Lawrence Seaway bypassed the city. Factories closed, docks fell silent, and the once-bustling canal basin was filled in and paved over. The waterfront that had birthed Buffalo's greatness became a graveyard of rusting machinery and empty lots. For decades, Buffalo turned its back on the river, and the once-proud grain elevators stood like forgotten monuments.

Opposite: Concrete Central Elevator, the farthest upstream on the Buffalo River.

Right: Scoopers hard at work unloading a shipment of grain.

27

Times Beach

From Sand, Shantytown, and Swimming Beach to Nature Preserve

Nestled where the Buffalo River meets Lake Erie, Times Beach has lived many lives. Once an Indigenous shoreline and sand spit reshaped for harbor construction, it became a shantytown of cottages and taverns, a briefly celebrated municipal bathing beach, then an industrial dredge dump, and finally–after decades of neglect–a reborn nature preserve. Few places along Buffalo's waterfront tell the city's story of ambition, decline, and renewal as vividly as this fifty-acre stretch of shoreline.

HARBOR BEGINNINGS AND SEAWALL SETTLEMENT

The origins of Times Beach lie in the early 19th century, when Buffalo's pioneers dug out a new outlet for Buffalo Creek to form a harbor. Breakwalls reshaped the shoreline, leaving a sandy spit that drew working families and laborers. By the late 1800s, the seawall neighborhood– sometimes called "Seawall Beach"was a dense cluster of cottages, taverns, seafood shacks, and boarding houses. Many residents were fishermen, grain scoopers, and dockworkers. Though poor, it was a lively community remembered by descendants as proud and tightly knit.

By the 1910s, city leaders viewed the district as an eyesore. In 1917, Buffalo launched a slum clearance campaign. Homes dating back to the 1840s were razed, taverns shuttered, and hundreds of residents displaced. The "Beachers," as they were known, were pushed aside as industry and new harbor plans took precedence. Within a generation, little remained of the neighborhood beyond memory.

THE DREAM OF A PUBLIC BEACH

In 1931, the Buffalo Times newspaper proposed transforming the abandoned sand spit into a free municipal bathing beach. Lifeguards were stationed that summer, and Buffalonians flocked to the lake. For a moment, Times Beach lived up to its name as the city's newest playground. Health officials even declared the water nearly as clean as a swimming pool.

But the optimism quickly faded. Within a few years, water tests revealed staggering levels of coliform bacteria–up to 200 times the safe limit. Runoff from the Buffalo River, combined with industrial waste and sewage, fouled the waters. By the mid-1930s, police discouraged swimming altogether. What might have been Buffalo's great public beach instead became another casualty of unchecked pollution.

Seawall Beach

FROM NEGLECT TO DUMPING GROUND

By the mid-20th century, Times Beach was described as a "weed-grown crescent." In 1952, the city acquired only a small portion for recreation, while the Niagara Frontier Port Authority eyed the rest for port expansion.

In the early 1970s, the U.S. Army Corps of Engineers turned the site into a confined disposal facility (CDF) for dredged sediment from the Buffalo River and Harbor. From 1972 to 1976, contaminated spoils–laden with heavy metals and industrial toxins–were pumped into the diked enclosure. Once dumping ceased, the area was fenced off and forgotten.

Ironically, neglect became the site's salvation. Left alone, cattails, shrubs, and young forests began colonizing the spoil piles. Birds returned to feed and nest. By the late 1970s, the Buffalo Ornithological Society recognized Times Beach as a promising habitat.

NATURE RECLAIMS THE SHORELINE

Through the 1980s and 1990s, birders, environmentalists, and community activists worked to preserve the accidental wetland. By 1987, scientists documented Times Beach as one of the largest and most diverse coastal wetlands left on Lake Erie's U.S. shore–a rare oasis in a region dominated by industry and concrete seawalls.

Advocates pressed for formal protection. After years of negotiations among the city, Erie County, and the Army Corps, the site was officially designated the Times Beach Nature Preserve in 2006. Trails, boardwalks, and bird blinds were built to balance access with conservation. Volunteers cleaned up trash, restored plantings, and monitored wildlife.

Above: Swimming at Times Beach until pollution and health concerns forced its closure.-1933

ECOLOGY AND IMPORTANCE

Today, the preserve encompasses roughly 50 acres of marsh, meadow, upland forest, and shoreline. It supports five distinct ecological zones and plays an outsized role in regional biodiversity. Over 240 bird species have been recorded here–one of the highest tallies in the Great Lakes. Warblers, shorebirds, raptors, waterfowl, and even bald eagles use the preserve as a migratory stopover. Mammals such as foxes, deer, and raccoons roam the meadows and groves. Monarch butterflies and native bees rely on its wildflowers for survival.

Times Beach also provides critical ecological services. Its wetlands filter pollutants, absorb storm water, and protect the shoreline against erosion. In an era of climate change and costly infrastructure projects, these natural systems save money while safeguarding public health.

ONGOING THREATS AND FUTURE PROSPECTS

Though formally protected, Times Beach remains vulnerable. Adjacent Outer Harbor lands controlled by the Niagara Frontier Transportation Authority are frequently targeted for high-rise development, commercial expansion, and new bridge proposals. Conservationists warn that such projects would fragment habitat and imperil the preserve's role as a migratory flyway. This tension reflects Buffalo's broader struggle over its waterfront identity: should it prioritize development, or preserve natural spaces as economic and cultural assets? For many, Times Beach proves that nature and heritage can coexist—and that ecological restoration can be as valuable as new construction.

EXPERIENCING THE PRESERVE

For visitors, Times Beach offers a quiet counterpoint to the bustle of downtown Buffalo. In winter, snow reveals tracks of foxes and rabbits, while chickadees flit through bare trees. Spring brings wildflowers and a chorus of migratory warblers. Summer hums with dragonflies and herons stalking the marshes, while autumn skies fill with hawks and geese.

Boardwalks and overlooks provide access without disturbing sensitive habitat. The site connects to the Shoreline Trail, linking it to Gallagher Beach, Tifft Nature Preserve, and the Small Boat Harbor. Bird watchers, families, and school groups now visit regularly, turning what was once a polluted dumping ground into an outdoor classroom.

A SYMBOL OF RENEWAL

Times Beach mirrors Buffalo's broader story—an arc of rise, decline, and rebirth. What began as a sandbar reshaped by harbor builders became a shantytown, then a short-lived beach, then an industrial waste site, and finally a thriving preserve. Its journey shows how forgotten places can be reclaimed, how nature persists even after abuse, and how communities can rally to protect what once seemed disposable.

Today, Times Beach is more than a park. It is a symbol of resilience, biodiversity, and the regenerative power of time and care. As Buffalo continues to reinvent its waterfront, the preserve offers both a lesson and a hope: that the future of the city lies not only in steel and concrete but also in marsh grass, migrating wings, and the quiet resilience of a place once nearly lost.

TIMES BEACH AND MIGRATORY BIRDS

Once a dredge dump turned ecological wasteland, Times Beach in Buffalo has been reborn as a haven for wildlife and birdwatchers alike. Restored as a nature preserve at the mouth of the Buffalo River, its wetlands now provide critical stopover habitat along the Atlantic Flyway. Each spring and fall, thousands of migratory birds—warblers, herons, sandpipers, and even bald eagles—pause here to feed and rest before continuing their long journeys. Raised boardwalks and observation platforms invite visitors to witness this seasonal spectacle, reminding Buffalo that urban waterfronts can be both wild sanctuary and community classroom.

Above: Rose Breasted Grossbeak

Oppossite: Times Beach as a recreational swimming area

31

Guiding Lights

For a city that rose to prominence because of its harbor, grain elevators, and canal connections, Buffalo's lighthouses stand as silent guardians of its maritime past. Buffalo's lighthouses represent the evolution of a working harbor that once ranked among the busiest on the Great Lakes.

THE BUFFALO MAIN LIGHTHOUSE

The oldest standing structure in the city, the Buffalo Main Lighthouse sits at the mouth of the Buffalo River where it meets Lake Erie. Built in 1833 of native limestone, the 61-foot tower replaced an earlier 1818 wooden beacon. Its placement was critical: this was the western terminus of the Erie Canal, and ships laden with grain and goods needed safe passage into Buffalo Harbor. The lighthouse once housed a third-order Fresnel lens, which projected light 15 miles over the lake. Retired from active service in 1914, it remains a treasured landmark within the Buffalo Harbor State Park and is listed on the National Register of Historic Places.

THE SOUTH BUFFALO LIGHTHOUSE

As the harbor expanded and breakwalls pushed farther into Lake Erie, a new light was needed to guide vessels around the shoals and piers of the Outer Harbor. The South Buffalo Lighthouse, completed in 1903, rose 44 feet in riveted steel plate and was painted white with a black lantern. For decades it guided lake freighters into the South Entrance Channel. Though automated in the 1960s, the light was deactivated in 1985 when changes to harbor traffic patterns made it obsolete. Restored by preservationists in the 1990s, it remains a sentinel on the breakwall.

Opposite: 1833 Buffalo Main Light

Left: A wooden structure was built on a pier west of the old lighthouse dubbed the "Chinaman's Light" as its roof resembled a Chinese coolie's hat and because it was also used to keep an eye out for illegal Chinese immigrants crossing over the Niagara River from Canada.

PART of LAKE ONTARIO

Niagara Fort

TANNAWANTO CREEK
▲▲▲▲▲▲

GENESEE RIVER

Fort Erie

BUFFALO CREEK
▲▲▲▲▲▲
▲▲▲▲▲▲▲

PART of LAKE ERIE

CATFISH CREEK
▲▲▲▲

CATTARAGUS Creek
▲▲▲▲
▲▲▲▲

LAKE CHAUTAUGHUR

ALLEGANY RIVER

34

Where Rivers Meet:
Buffalo's Transformations Along the Erie Canal

*The Erie Canal's legacy in Buffalo is not a single story of triumph,
but a tapestry woven of displacement and opportunity, inequity and innovation,
hardship and hope. To honor the river's past is to acknowledge all who lived
along its banks, and to recognize that the waters still carry their echoes.*

REMEMBERING THE MANY VOICES

Today, as kayakers paddle past restored grain elevators and walkers trace the boardwalks of Canalside, it is worth remembering that the Buffalo River is layered with stories. They are stories of the Haudenosaunee who named the waters, of Black laborers who loaded the docks, of women who kept households afloat, and of immigrants who reshaped a city.

Long before surveyors drew lines on maps or engineers envisioned a waterway to the West, the Buffalo River wound quietly through forests, wetlands, and marshes. For the Haudenosaunee Confederacy–particularly the Seneca Nation–the river was both a homeland and a lifeline. Its bends and oxbows held spawning fish, its banks nurtured corn and squash, and its waters carried stories passed down through generations. The Seneca word for the place, Tehoseroron, meant "where

there is a place of the bass." It was a name rooted in relationship, not possession.

The opening of the Erie Canal in 1825 did not just move goods; it redefined ownership. For the Haudenosaunee, the canal's celebration in Buffalo was less about progress and more about loss.

A SACRED PLACE

Buffalo Creek was once a vital homeland for the Seneca Nation, the "Keepers of the Western Door" of the Haudenosaunee (Iroquois Confederacy). The Seneca gained control of this area in the 17th century, establishing it as an important site of cultural, political, and spiritual life. For generations, Buffalo Creek stood not only as a home but also as a symbol of the Nation's sovereignty.

DISPLACEMENT AND LOSS

As the United States expanded westward, pressure mounted on Indigenous nations to surrender their lands. Through coercion, manipulation, and unfair treaty negotiations, the Seneca were forced into a cycle of loss. Buffalo Creek lands, once central to the community, gradually slipped away under these pressures. In time, the land was transformed into what became the growing city of Buffalo.

THE 1838 "CROOKED" TREATY

The most infamous agreement was the Treaty of Buffalo Creek, signed in 1838 under the shadow of the U.S. Indian Removal Act. Often called the "crooked treaty," it was negotiated in bad faith, with evidence of fraud and manipulation. The treaty called for the sale of Seneca and other Haudenosaunee lands in New York and the relocation of these nations to the Kansas Territory. Many Seneca opposed the treaty, recognizing it as a direct threat to their survival and autonomy.

THE 1842 TREATY: A PARTIAL REPRIEVE

Resistance by Seneca leaders, combined with public outcry over the injustices of the earlier treaty, led to a new agreement in 1842. This treaty represented a compromise: the Seneca formally ceded the valuable Buffalo Creek Reservation but retained their lands at Cattaraugus and Allegany. These remaining territories provided a foothold for the Seneca people to continue their lives in Western New York, avoiding the total displacement that federal officials had envisioned. The canal's success was inseparable from the erasure of older geographies of belonging.

BLACK LABOR AND ASPIRATIONS

The canal also carved space for Black laborers. Many formerly enslaved people came north following the current of the canal itself. In Buffalo, they dug, hauled, and loaded cargo at the terminus docks, often for wages lower than their white counterparts.

Buffalo's waterfront and surrounding areas hold a significant legacy of early Black history, from pioneer Joseph "Black Joe" Hodge in the late 1700s operating a trading post at Canalside, to the crucial role the Erie Canal and waterfront played in the Underground Railroad. The canal offered more than hardship. Its waters formed an artery of freedom. Black families, aided by abolitionists and sympathetic sailors, found pathways to Canada via canal boats connecting to the Niagara River.

The area became a hub for freedom seekers and abolitionists, with Black residents establishing businesses, churches like the Michigan Street Baptist Church (1831), and community organizations on Michigan Street, contributing to the development of early Black civil rights movements.

Black Americans found work along the waterfront as sailors, stewards, and cooks. During the late 1800s, Black dockworkers were sometimes used as strikebreakers against union efforts, leading to violent conflicts, including a 1891 riot where Black workers were targeted and attacked.

A number of black owned businesses establish at a 3-story building known as the Union Block at Canalside. The area is well known as a magnet for

Left: Michigan Street Church

Opposite: Haudenosaunee Village

vice, with as many as 60% of buildings serving as brothels.

One of the more colorful establishments is Dug's Dive, operated by William Douglas, an escaped slave from Tennessee. Located below sea level, the bar is a literal "dive" one could not stand upright in. Douglas reportedly assists freedom seekers on the underground railroad.

WOMEN AT THE WATER'S EDGE

Women's contributions to the Erie Canal are often invisible, yet they are everywhere in the record. They ran boardinghouses for immigrant workers, washed their clothes, and tended their injuries. In taverns along the Buffalo River, women brewed beer and kept accounts while their husbands labored on the towpaths. Some women themselves became canal boat captains–managing crews, navigating locks, and earning reputations as tough as any man's.

Closer to the river, Indigenous and immigrant women kept households that were often precarious. Floods and disease swept through shantytowns built too close to the water. Women shouldered the burdens of survival–drawing water, cooking for labor gangs, raising children in overcrowded quarters. Their stories reveal the canal not just as a technological achievement, but as a human landscape marked by resilience.

IMMIGRANT COMMUNITIES ON THE RISE

Buffalo's rapid growth owed much to immigrants who saw in the canal both opportunity and struggle. Irish workers, many fleeing famine, wielded shovels and picks to dig the waterway itself. Later, German immigrants brought skills in brewing and milling that clustered along the Buffalo River. Polish and Italian families soon followed, settling near the grain elevators that rose like cathedrals on the horizon.

Each community carried with it traditions, languages, and foods that reshaped Buffalo into a polyglot city. Yet each also bore the sting of prejudice. Signs that read "No Irish Need Apply" or derisive caricatures in newspapers reminded immigrants that the canal's prosperity was stratified. Still, through unions, churches, and neighborhood associations, these communities forged solidarity and left indelible cultural marks on Buffalo.

Dante Place, 1910 - photograph by Wilbur H. Porterfield.

INNOVATION ON THE WATERFRONT

The Erie Canal was not merely a ditch of water–it was a laboratory of innovation. At Buffalo's harbor, engineers built breakwaters to calm the lake's waves, dredged the river's mouth to handle deeper vessels, and developed new hoisting systems for grain. By the 1840s, Joseph Dart's invention of the steam-powered grain elevator transformed the waterfront into one of the busiest ports in North America.

A CITY TRANSFORMED

Within a generation, Buffalo was unrecognizable. What had been a small frontier village in 1820 became a bustling city by mid-century, its population multiplying nearly tenfold. Canal boats brought flour, lumber, whiskey, and salt to the lake port; railroads soon added another layer of connectivity. The Buffalo River, once a quiet fishery of the Seneca, became lined with iron foundries, tanneries, and elevators.

For the Haudenosaunee, the river's transformation was a reminder of promises broken but also of enduring stewardship. For Black residents, it was both opportunity and a launching point toward freedom. For women, it was the site of invisible labor that kept families alive. For immigrants, it was the entry point into the American industrial economy.

Above: The Canal District at the foot of Main Street.

THE INFECTED DISTRICT

Buffalo's waterfront has cycled through prosperity, vice, decline, and rebirth. Canalside ties those threads together, making the site not only a place of recreation but also a reminder of the city's endurance. What was once called the "worst slum" in the city is now its most vibrant public square.

The Canal Era

When the Erie Canal opened in 1825, Buffalo changed overnight. The Commercial Slip at the foot of Main Street became the western gateway to the state's grand water highway. Packet boats docked daily, unloading passengers, goods, and ambitions from across New York and beyond. Grain elevators rose, warehouses multiplied, and the town quickly turned into a city.

The area around the slip became known as the Canal District. It was noisy, crowded, and profitable. Thousands of immigrants–many of them Irish–arrived to dig, unload, and haul. Boarding houses, saloons, and shops catered to this new labor force. For Buffalo, the canal was a ticket to prosperity, but the waterfront was also where the city's rough edges were most visible.

The Infected District

By the 1830s, Buffalo's canal neighborhood had gained notoriety. Known as "the Infected District," "the Hooks," or simply Canal Street, it became infamous as one of the roughest waterfronts in the nation. It was often called "the most evil square mile in America."

A walk down Canal Street revealed dozens of taverns, theaters, boarding houses, and brothels, many crammed together on narrow blocks. Reformers tried to quantify its reputation. The Christian Homestead Association produced a large wall chart that

Opposite: Commercial Slip and the foot of Commercial Street-1868

Right: It's said that many a drunken sailor were robbed and unceremoniously dumped into the Canal for spontaneous swimming lessons. This painting is located at Pearl Street Grill.

41

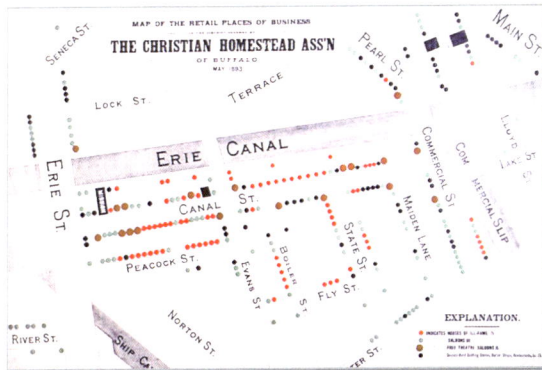

mapped out every saloon and house of prostitution, using red dots to make the scale unmistakable. Their survey counted 108 saloons, 19 "free theater" saloons, and 75 brothels within the compact area. The report noted another 75 small businesses–second-hand clothing shops, barber shops, restaurants–serving the same clientele.

Vice here was not hidden. Saloons stayed open all night. Sailors spent their wages quickly, and the women of Canal Street played active roles not just as prostitutes but also as fighters. Arrest reports show them charged with brawling, knifings, and even murder.

At the same time, poverty was as defining as vice. Canal Street lay within Buffalo's 19th Ward, which had the city's highest concentration of tenement housing by the 1890s. Italian immigrants in particular crowded into decaying, unsafe structures. Tenements intended for 100 people often housed over 1000, with the worst conditions concentrated in the canal area. Investigators described blocks where water closets "were too filthy for use," and families of five or six slept in rooms barely ten feet square. Poor sanitation fueled outbreaks of cholera and other diseases, reinforcing the neighborhood's label as "infected."

REFORM AND DISAPPEARANCE

Through the late 19th century, reformers tried to erase the district by renaming it. Canal Street became Dante Place, as if an Italian poet's name could cleanse its reputation. Police raids periodically shuttered saloons and brothels, only for new ones to appear.

City leaders eventually attacked the neighborhood physically. The Hamburg Canal was filled in, the Commercial Slip covered with cinders and rubble, and new buildings rose on top of the buried waterway. By the early 20th century, the geography of Buffalo's original waterfront was literally erased.

THE MEMORIAL AUDITORIUM

In 1939, Buffalo built Memorial Auditorium–the Aud–on the site of the old slip. For the next six decades, the Aud defined the area. It was home to the Buffalo Bisons basketball team, then to the Buffalo Sabres hockey franchise. It hosted circuses, professional wrestling, political rallies, and concerts.

DECLINE AND DEMOLITION

By the 1990s, the Aud had become outdated. The Sabres moved into a new arena, and the building sat vacant. In 2009, after years of debate, the Aud was demolished. What remained was a large, empty tract at the city's front door–a place heavy with history but stripped of identity. That vacancy set the stage for a new era.

THE RESTORATION OF THE SLIP

The first step was reopening the Commercial Slip itself. In the early 2000s, the slip was excavated, refilled with water, and lined with new timber wharves. The Central Wharf was reconstructed as a public boardwalk, with interpretive panels and tours explaining the site's role in Buffalo's development. What began as a heritage project quickly grew into a broader vision: a mixed-use waterfront space that combined history with recreation.

Above: 1893 Map from the Christian Homestead Association of the "Houses of Ill-Fame" in the Canal District (Source: Rare Book Room of the Buffalo and Erie County Public Library)

Opposite:"Buffalo gals won't you come out tonight" is a reference to female performers and prostitutes from the Canal district in the 19th century, who worked in the bars, brothels, and concert halls that catered to the large concentration of men from the Erie Canal workforce. The song itself became a popular minstrel show tune.

Canalside Today

Few places capture Buffalo's renaissance as vividly as Canalside. Once a derelict stretch of industrial waterfront along the Buffalo River, it has become the city's front porch–a gathering place, an entertainment district, and a living museum of Buffalo's history. Today, Canalside is the jewel of the Queen City's waterfront crown, welcoming over a million visitors annually and hosting more than 1,000 events each year.

THE BOARDWALK AND CENTRAL WHARF

The heart of Canalside is its expansive boardwalk along the river. Strolling here, visitors can take in sweeping views, enjoy live music, rent bikes, or hop on a harbor cruise. Summer evenings bring concerts, outdoor yoga classes, and family games to the Central Wharf, while food trucks and waterfront dining make it easy to linger. In winter, the recreated Erie Canal becomes the 35,000-square-foot Ice at Canalside, where skating, curling, pond hockey, and even whimsical ice bikes turn the district into a cold-weather festival.

THE LONGSHED AND LIVING HISTORY

At the northern end of the Wharf stands the Longshed, a striking two-story timber building inspired by early 19th-century warehouses. Inside, the Buffalo Maritime Center spent three years constructing a replica of the Seneca Chief, the packet boat that carried Governor DeWitt Clinton on the "Wedding of the Waters" voyage celebrating the Erie Canal's grand opening in 1825. Visitors could watch shipwrights at work, and even volunteer, making the Longshed a hands-on link between Buffalo's canal-era past and its 21st-century rebirth.

Left to Right: The Solar-Powered Buffalo Heritage Carousel | Bike Ferry to the Outer Harbor | Ice skating on the frozen, rewatered canal | Explore & More - The Ralph C. Wilson, Jr. Children's Museum- with seven play zones and three educational studios that are used to tell the unique story of Western New York.

SPORTS, FOOD, AND FUN

Directly across the street, LECOM Harborcenter anchors Canalside as a sports destination. With two NHL-sized rinks, it hosts tournaments and training camps that dr-aw hockey players from around the world. For fans, the Southern Tier Brewery combines pub fare with a wall of 70 televisions–topped by a 38-foot screen for the biggest games. Families can explore the Ralph C. Wilson Explore & More Children's Museum, a state-of-the-art space for interactive play and learning. Steps away, Liberty Hound restaurant overlooks the water, while Clinton's Dish serves up ice cream cones perfect for sunset on one of the district's signature Adirondack "sunset chairs."

A HUB OF CULTURE AND HERITAGE

Canalside is also a gateway to Buffalo's larger waterfront. Next door lies the Buffalo and Erie County Naval & Military Park, the nation's largest inland naval park, where visitors tour historic ships including the cruiser USS Little Rock and destroyer USS The Sullivans. A short walk brings you to the Erie Basin Marina, with its observation tower and flower gardens, or to the historic 1833 Buffalo Lighthouse guarding the river's mouth. From the Queen City Bike Ferry, passengers can cross to the Outer Harbor for fishing, birdwatching, and miles of hiking and biking trails.

A SYMBOL OF BUFFALO'S REVIVAL

Once a place of neglect, Canalside now showcases Buffalo's resilience and pride. It sits at the 1825 terminus of the Erie Canal–the very spot where the city rose to prominence as a transportation and industrial powerhouse. Today, that history is honored not just in exhibits and replicas, but in the energy of a district alive with concerts, festivals, history tours, and year-round recreation.

Canalside is no longer just a waterfront park. It is Buffalo's front porch–welcoming locals and visitors alike to relax, play, learn, and rediscover the city's enduring connection to the water that built it.

Left and Right: The Boardwalk at Canalside

47

Buffalo and Erie County Naval and Military Park

Opened in 1979, the Buffalo and Erie County Naval & Military Park is the largest inland naval park in the United States and a cornerstone of Buffalo's waterfront. Located along the Buffalo River at Canalside, the park preserves and interprets military history through a remarkable collection of ships, aircraft, and exhibits.

The park's centerpiece is its floating fleet, which includes the cruiser USS Little Rock, the destroyer USS The Sullivans, and the submarine USS Croaker. Visitors can step aboard these historic vessels, exploring everything from command bridges to cramped crew quarters. Each ship carries its own story–The Sullivans, for example, honors five brothers who lost their lives together during World War II.

On shore, the park offers a museum filled with military artifacts, rotating exhibits, and interactive displays that honor service across all branches of the armed forces. The outdoor grounds feature a solemn array of monuments and memorials, including tributes to local Medal of Honor recipients and the nation's wars and conflicts.

More than just a museum, the Naval Park serves as a living memorial and a place of education, reflection, and civic pride. It connects Buffalo's waterfront revival to a larger story of national service and sacrifice.

Right: USS The Sullivans,
Opposite: Submarine USS Croaker

EXPERIENCING BUFFALO FROM THE WATER

There is no better way to experience Buffalo's waterfront than by getting out on the water itself. These leisurely cruises across Lake Erie and the Buffalo River reveals its beauty best when the sun is on your face and the breeze comes off the lake.

MOONDANCE CAT *(Right:)*
For more than 36 years, the Moondance Cat has offered a lively sailing experience aboard its 65-passenger catamaran. With twin hulls connected by a wide party deck, a full-service bar, and room to mingle, this vessel is perfect for a summer evening on the water.

SPIRIT OF BUFFALO *(Opposite:)*
Step back in time aboard the Spirit of Buffalo, a 73-foot topsail schooner with distinctive red sails. Passengers can help hoist the rigging or simply relax and enjoy skyline views and unforgettable sunsets over Lake Erie.

MISS BUFFALO *(Below:)*
A tradition for more than 50 years, the Miss Buffalo provides narrated tours of the Inner and Outer Harbors, showcasing Buffalo's working waterfront and natural scenery from the sailor's perspective.

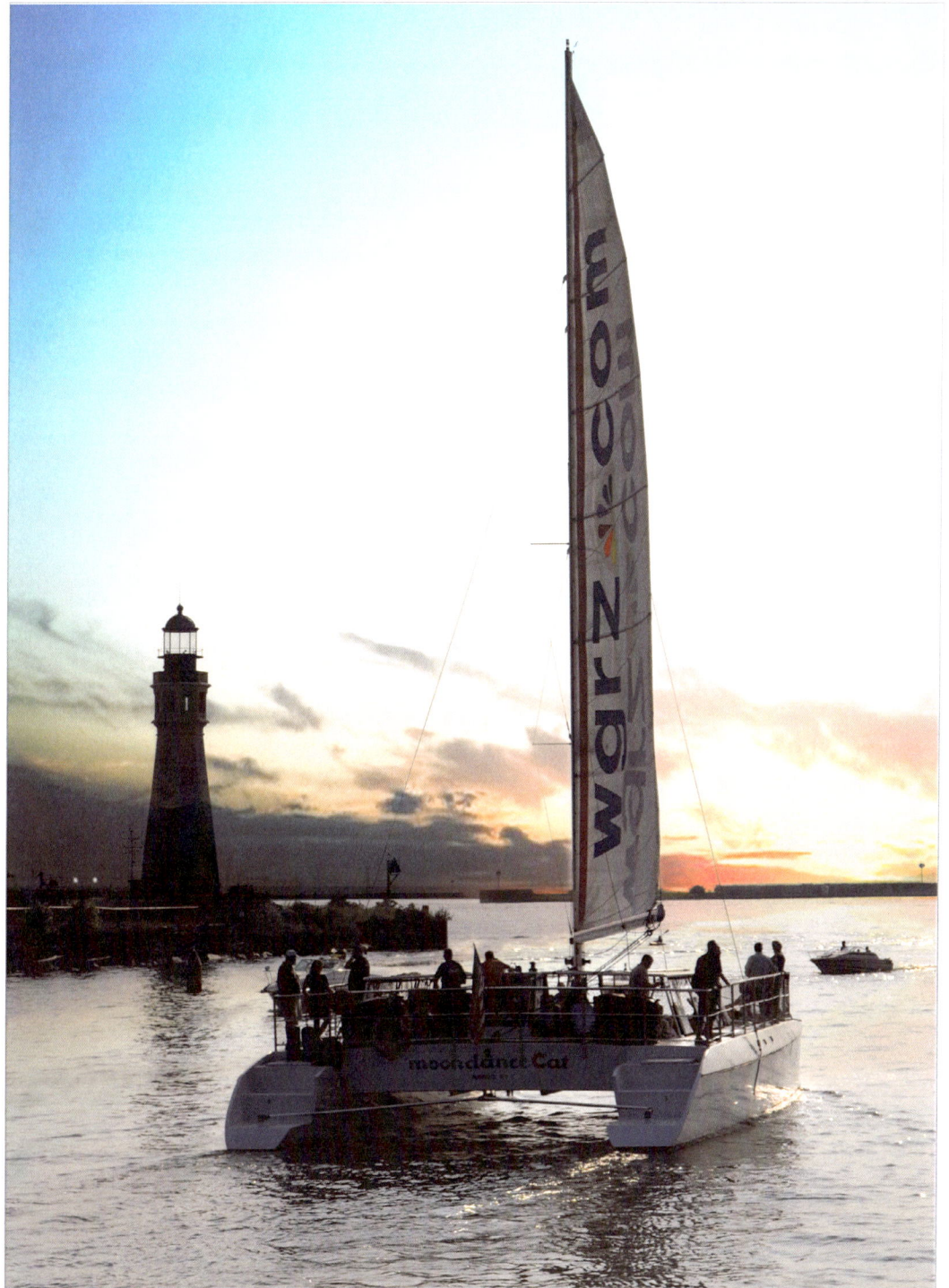

ERIE BASIN HARBOR

The Erie Basin Marina, today one of Buffalo's most iconic waterfront destinations, began with a far more utilitarian purpose. Originally constructed as a breakwater and commercial slip at the mouth of the Buffalo River, it was designed to blunt Lake Erie's powerful storm surges. For decades it was nothing more than a protective barrier, not even connected to the mainland. That changed with a major lakefront improvement project between 1970 and 1973, when roads, walkways, marina slips, a tower, and support buildings were added.

A hidden design flourish makes the site even more distinctive: when viewed from the air, from the observation deck of Buffalo City Hall, or even by passing pilots, the marina reveals itself to be laid out in the shape of a giant buffalo. This creative touch gave the site symbolic as well as functional value.

Beyond serving boaters with over 1,000 slips, the marina has blossomed into a neighborhood of its own. Condominiums, offices, and restaurants bring year-round activity. Its landscaped test gardens are a quiet gem, offering colorful seasonal displays and experimental plantings. Once just a breakwater, the Erie Basin Marina now embodies Buffalo's waterfront renaissance—a community gathering place, a boating hub, and a living symbol of the city itself.

The Front,
N. Y. Central Bridge, Buffalo, N. Y.

BUFFALO'S WATERFRONT PARKS

Buffalo's parks have always been shaped by their relationship to water. From Olmsted's 19th-century vision of scenic riverfront overlooks to today's bold reimagining of downtown's largest lakefront green space, the city's waterfront parks tell the story of both preservation and renewal. Buffalo's waterfront parks continue to anchor neighborhoods, inspire pride, and ensure that the city's defining natural asset, the water, remains central to its public life.

FRONT PARK

Originally called The Front, Front Park was once the most popular recreational destination in Buffalo and a prominent city icon. As with Delaware Park and MLK Jr. Park, Frederick Law Olmsted himself chose the location, but with a distinctive purpose in mind. Designed between 1868 and 1870 by Olmsted & Vaux, the 32-acre park sits at Porter and Busti Avenues, overlooking Lake Erie and the mouth of the Niagara River.

The park's most striking feature is its semi-circular terrace, carefully positioned to command panoramic views of the water. With the Niagara River as backdrop, the terrace became a dramatic setting for civic gatherings and leisurely enjoyment. Olmsted intended Front Park to balance recreation with spectacle, designing open lawns for baseball and cricket–games he considered democratic because "anyone could play." His 1871 plan also included a playground, graveled terrace, grassy commons, and a proposed music stand for concerts.

Monuments and features soon enriched the park. A statue of Commodore Oliver Hazard Perry recalls his naval victory on Lake Erie during the War of 1812, while the park's historic shelter house was recently restored. The Parrott Rifles, Civil War–era artillery pieces, were also restored and returned to their terrace placement in 2013.

Yet, intrusions reshaped Olmsted's masterpiece. The opening of the Peace Bridge in 1925 carved away parkland, and highway expansions further compromised its integrity. Once a sweeping overlook, the Front is now hemmed in by traffic and lost its scenic relationship to the river. Still, its essential elements remain, reminding visitors of Olmsted's vision and Buffalo's early pride in its waterfront.

RIVERSIDE PARK

Riverside Park, completed in 1898, was the final addition to Buffalo's Olmsted system and the only park designed directly on the Niagara River. Located in the city's northwest corner, Riverside was conceived as a neighborhood gathering space with strong connections to the water. Its curving paths, wooded groves, and meadows once led directly to the riverbank. Though shoreline industry later altered its edges, Riverside has endured as a community anchor.

Today, the park offers a wide array of amenities: playgrounds, a pool, ballfields, and picnic groves, all maintained by the Buffalo Olmsted Parks Conservancy. Seasonal events keep the park lively, from summer sports to community celebrations, sustaining Olmsted's vision of an accessible, family-friendly riverfront.

RALPH WILSON PARK

Ralph Wilson Park–formerly LaSalle Park–represents the boldest new chapter in Buffalo's waterfront story. Stretching 90 acres along Lake Erie just south of downtown, it is the city's largest waterfront park. For decades, the park functioned primarily as open athletic fields in the shadow of the Skyway. In 2018, a $100 million gift from the Ralph C. Wilson Jr. Foundation set the stage for a complete transformation.

Opposite: A postcard of people strolling along "The Front" (Front Park)

THE PEACE BRIDGE

Spanning the Niagara River between Buffalo, New York, and Fort Erie, Ontario, the Peace Bridge has been a symbol of international connection since it opened on June 1, 1927. Construction began in 1925 to relieve congestion at the International Railway Bridge and to accommodate the rise of automobiles. When completed, the five-arch steel structure stretched nearly a mile, linking the United States and Canada at one of the busiest border crossings in North America.

The bridge was dedicated in a grand ceremony attended by dignitaries from both nations, including the Prince of Wales (later King Edward VIII). Its name commemorated over a century of peace between the U.S. and Canada following the War of 1812. From the start, the Peace Bridge embodied not only engineering achievement but also diplomatic goodwill.

Today, more than 5 million vehicles cross it annually, carrying commuters, tourists, and international trade. Its striking steelwork remains a defining feature of Buffalo's skyline, visible from Front Park, the Erie Basin Marina, and the Niagara River itself. Though expansions of the bridge and plaza have claimed sections of Olmsted's historic Front Park, the Peace Bridge remains a vital gateway between two nations.

Efforts are ongoing to modernize the bridge and its U.S. plaza while balancing efficiency with environmental and community concerns. Nearly a century after its opening, the Peace Bridge continues to serve as both a practical artery of commerce and a powerful symbol of friendship across borders.

Right: At night, the Peace Bridge becomes a glowing landmark as waves of colored lights ripple across its steel arches. The shifting hues, sometimes bold, sometimes subtle, reflect on the Niagara River below, symbolizing both the vibrant spirit of Buffalo and Fort Erie and the enduring friendship between the U.S. and Canada.

56

FORT ERIE, ONTARIO

Perched at the head of the Niagara River where it meets Lake Erie, Fort Erie, Ontario, has long served as both gateway and battleground. Its strategic location made it a natural crossing point between Canada and the United States, and today it remains a border community linked to Buffalo, New York, by the Peace Bridge. But the town's story is inseparable from its namesake stronghold: Old Fort Erie.

The British first constructed the fort in 1764, making it the first British fort built on the Canadian side of the Niagara River. Over the years it was expanded, but its most dramatic chapter came during the War of 1812. In 1814, American forces captured Old Fort Erie and used it as a base for their Niagara campaign. The fort endured one of the bloodiest sieges in Canadian history, when British troops attempted to retake it in a prolonged and brutal assault. By November, the Americans withdrew, and the fort was left in ruins, a powerful reminder of the high cost of the conflict.

Today, Old Fort Erie has been reconstructed and serves as a living history site operated by the Niagara Parks Commission. Visitors can walk its ramparts, tour barracks and powder magazines, and watch reenactments of the 1814 siege. Together with the surrounding town–home to beaches, waterfront trails, and a proud community–Fort Erie offers a blend of natural beauty and layered history, standing as both border town and keeper of wartime memory.

Left: Old Fort Erie stands as a solemn sentinel, preserving stories of war, resilience, and one of Canada's bloodiest battlefields.

Right: Mather Arch in Fort Erie is a stone gateway honoring peace and the enduring bond between Canada and the United States.

SHIPBUILDING IN BLACK ROCK

Before Buffalo's rise as a Great Lakes powerhouse, Black Rock–its rival settlement just upriver–was a vital shipbuilding center. The east bank of the Niagara River, sheltered by Squaw Island (now Unity Island), offered calmer waters than the exposed mouth of Buffalo Creek. In the early 1800s, when control of the lakes meant both commerce and security, this natural harbor gave Black Rock a decisive advantage.

Black Rock's yards turned out schooners, brigs, and, most famously, the side-wheel steamer Walk-in-the-Water. Launched in 1818, it was the first steamboat to navigate Lake Erie, marking a bold new era of powered navigation and opening the Great Lakes frontier to greater movement of goods and people. During the War of 1812, the same boatyards pivoted to military needs. Ships were repaired, armed, and refitted to support Commodore Oliver Hazard Perry's fleet before the decisive Battle of Lake Erie. Local timber, regional iron, and frontier craftsmanship combined to meet the urgent wartime demand.

Even after Buffalo secured the Erie Canal terminus in 1825 and eclipsed its neighbor, Black Rock retained its shipbuilding identity. During the mid-19th century, the yards produced canal boats, scows, and trading craft that supplied both sides of the border. With the Civil War, Union supply lines made use of the Niagara frontier's shipbuilding and transport links, further tying Black Rock's maritime industry to national events.

Though the yards eventually gave way to railroads and warehouses, the legacy of Black Rock's shipbuilders endures. Along its waterfront, one can still imagine the sounds of saws and hammers shaping the vessels that carried both commerce and conflict across the inland seas.

Opposite: Robert McGreely's painting "The Walk in the Water" captures the drama of the first steamboat to sail Lake Erie, launched from Buffalo in 1818. With billowing smoke and paddle wheels cutting through the waves, the artwork conveys both the daring spirit of early navigation and the promise of a new era of commerce and connection across the Great Lakes.

Right: Map of Blackrock shipbuilding area

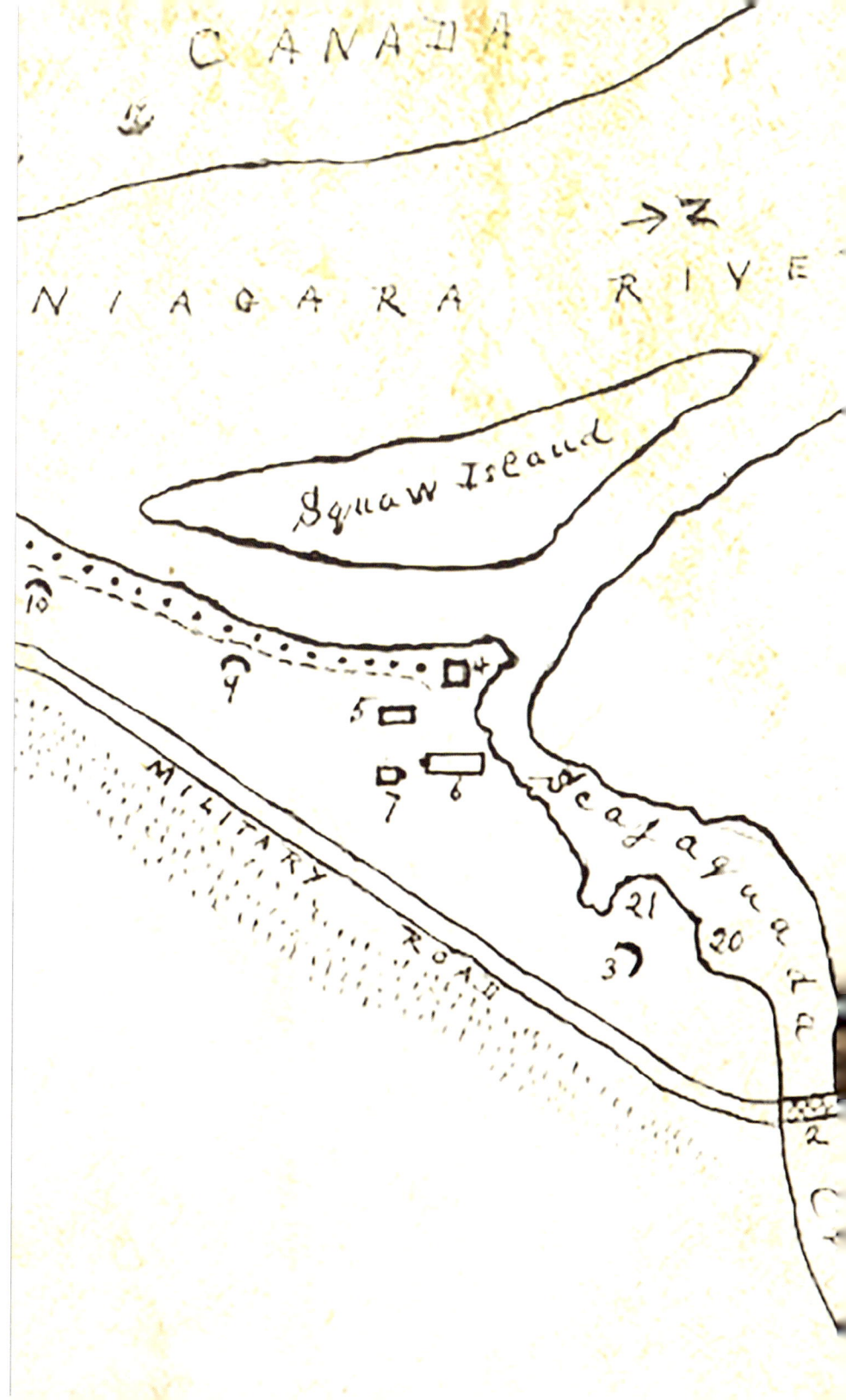

BUFFALO VS. BLACK ROCK
The Battle for the Erie Canal Terminus

When the Erie Canal was conceived in the early 19th century, one question overshadowed all others: where would it meet Lake Erie? The stakes were enormous. The chosen community would become the western gateway to the Great Lakes and the American West, reaping vast economic benefits. The contest quickly narrowed to two contenders–Buffalo and Black Rock.

At the time, Buffalo was a modest frontier village with fewer than 2,000

residents. It had little infrastructure, no real harbor, and a shallow shoreline blocked by a sandbar. Lake winds were fierce, and vessels struggled to reach the shore. By comparison, Black Rock seemed far better positioned. Its name came from a 100-foot outcropping that formed a natural wharf. The settlement boasted a sheltered harbor protected by Bird and Squaw Islands and had already developed into a busier port than Buffalo.

Black Rock's most forceful advocate was Peter Porter, a lawyer, politician, and entrepreneur. Porter controlled trade along the Niagara River and stood to gain immensely if the canal ended there. He even devised a solution to the river's powerful current: teams of oxen, nicknamed the "Horn Breeze," hauled vessels upriver to reach Lake Erie. Black Rock also launched the "Walk-in-the-Water", the first steamboat on Lake Erie, underscoring its maritime ambitions.

Buffalo, however, had determined champions of its own. Joseph Ellicott, who had laid out the village, and Samuel Wilkeson, a civic leader, lobbied fiercely for harbor improvements. In 1819, engineer William Peacock, a friend of Ellicott's, surveyed the competing sites and recommended Buffalo—provided a pier was built into the lake to shelter a harbor. This tipped momentum toward Buffalo, though debates raged for years.

The Canal Commission and state engineers changed their recommendations multiple times between 1819 and 1822. At one point, Black Rock seemed poised to win; at another, Buffalo reclaimed the advantage. Engineers like David Thomas argued that Black Rock's improvements would be prohibitively expensive, while Buffalo's shallow shoreline could be transformed with man-made structures. Meanwhile, storms damaged Black Rock's harbor and even destroyed the "Walk-in-the-Water," further undermining its prospects.

By 1822, the decision was largely settled in Buffalo's favor, though Black Rock continued to lobby fiercely. The final blow came in 1825, when an "independent canal" section was built parallel to the Niagara River, bypassing Black Rock altogether. That spring, flooding destroyed its harbor entirely, erasing any lingering hopes.

On October 26, 1825, Governor DeWitt Clinton led a flotilla from Buffalo aboard the Seneca Chief, beginning the famous "Wedding of the Waters" journey that opened the Erie Canal. Buffalo's designation as the western terminus transformed it almost overnight into a boomtown, launching its

rise as a major American city.

Black Rock, by contrast, entered a long decline, eventually being annexed into Buffalo in 1853. Yet its role in the fierce contest for the canal remains a vivid chapter in Western New York history—a reminder that geography, politics, and sheer determination can shape the fate of entire communities.

Opposite: The boat traffic in the busy Buffalo Harbor
Above: Patrick O'Brien's The Battle of Lake Erie vividly recreates Commodore Oliver Hazard Perry's 1813 naval victory, a turning point in the War of 1812. With cannon fire, billowing smoke, and ships locked in close combat, O'Brien's dramatic brushwork captures both the chaos of battle and the resolve that secured American control of Lake Erie.

SHORELINE TRAIL

LOWER RIVER

→ **Devil's Hole Stairs**

↑ **Gorgeview**
Whirlpool State Park
DeVeaux Woods
State Park

DEVIL'S HOLE STATE PARK

HISTORY

THE NIAGARA RIVER GREENWAY

-The Niagara River Greenway is a bold vision to reconnect communities with one of the world's great waterways. Established in 2004 by the New York State Legislature, the Greenway is a 36-mile corridor of parks, trails, and conservation lands stretching from Lake Erie, through the Niagara River, to Lake Ontario. Its mission is simple but ambitious: to create a continuous, accessible, and sustainable system of green spaces that celebrates the river's natural beauty, cultural history, and recreational potential.

Funded in part by the New York Power Authority through a settlement tied to the Niagara Power Project, the Greenway Commission oversees planning and partnerships. Dozens of municipalities, nonprofits, and community groups contribute projects that range from shoreline habitat restoration and fishing access to bike paths and heritage interpretation.

For residents and visitors alike, the Greenway offers multiple ways to experience the river. Cyclists can ride the Shoreline Trail from Buffalo's Outer Harbor to Niagara Falls, while walkers and birders explore parks and wetlands reclaimed from industrial lands. Historical markers highlight the region's Indigenous heritage, the War of 1812, and the Underground Railroad.

Still a work in progress, the Greenway is gradually stitching together a riverfront that had long been fragmented by industry and infrastructure. When complete, it will provide an uninterrupted ribbon of green space, connecting neighborhoods, preserving ecosystems, and celebrating the Niagara's role as both natural wonder and cultural lifeline.

Grand Island

Grand Island, the largest island in the Niagara River, sits quietly between Buffalo and Niagara Falls. At 33 square miles, it has long been a place of both strategic importance and natural beauty. To the Haudenosaunee, the island was a hunting ground, rich with deer, fish, and waterfowl. Known to the Seneca as Ni-ga-ga-rah-ga-ha, it was considered a shared resource rather than a permanent settlement.

During the 19th century, Grand Island nearly became something much larger. In 1824, President John Quincy Adams authorized its sale as part of federal land policy, and early speculators envisioned a grand city to rival Buffalo. Later, in the 1850s, the island was even proposed as the site of a Jewish homeland by Mordecai Noah, who imagined a utopian refuge called "Ararat." Though that dream never materialized, the episode remains one of the more fascinating "what-ifs" in American history.

Grand Island eventually developed as a rural retreat. In the late 19th and early 20th centuries, summer cottages and resorts drew city residents seeking fresh air and river breezes. Agriculture and dairy farming also flourished. By mid-century, the construction of the Grand Island Bridges and the New York State Thruway connected the island more closely to Buffalo and Niagara Falls, spurring suburban development.

Today, Grand Island balances residential life with parkland. Beaver Island State Park, Buckhorn Island Preserve, and miles of shoreline trails highlight its enduring connection to the natural environment, a green respite in the heart of the Niagara frontier.

Opposite: The beach at Beaver Island State Park

Left: The South Grand Island Bridge is a pair of twin two-lane truss arch bridges spanning the Niagara River between Tonawanda and Grand Island.

THE TONAWANDA'S
Twin Cities on the Canal and River

North Tonawanda and Tonawanda–collectively known as "the Tonawandas"–sit at the point where the Niagara River meets the Erie Canal. Though separated by the creek, the two cities have long shared industries, traditions, and fortunes, bound together by water and history.

EARLY SETTLEMENT AND THE CANAL ERA

The word "Tonawanda" comes from a Seneca term often translated as "swift waters," an apt name for the fast current of the Niagara. In the early 19th century, farming settlements appeared along the creek, but it was the opening of the Erie Canal in 1825 that transformed the region. Positioned where lake and canal met, the Tonawandas became ideal transshipment ports. Timber floated east from the Midwest arrived here by lake schooner and canal barge, and by the late 1800s the Tonawandas were celebrated as the "Lumber Capital of the Northeast." Towering piles of pine, hemlock, and oak lined the waterfront, destined for houses, ships, and factories across the growing United States.

INDUSTRY AND COMMUNITY LIFE

Lumber supported a vast network of sawmills, planing mills, and eventually paper plants that turned the timber trade into a full industrial economy. Immigrant labor–German, Polish, and Italian–powered this growth, bringing with it cultural institutions, churches, and taverns. Oliver Street in North Tonawanda became the beating heart of working-class life. Its lively bars provided not just a drink after long shifts in the yards and factories, but also neighborhood centers where politics, union drives, and friendships flourished.

Herschell Carrousel Factory

Even as Buffalo overshadowed its neighbors, the Tonawandas retained an industrial identity. Paper mills, boatbuilding yards, and machine shops added diversity, keeping the waterfront busy with commerce well into the 20th century.

THE HERSCHELL CARROUSEL FACTORY

One of the Tonawandas' most distinctive contributions to American industry was the Herschell Carrousel Factory in North Tonawanda. Established in the late 19th century, it grew into the world's leading producer of hand-carved wooden carousels and amusement rides. From here, brightly painted horses, lions, and chariots were shipped to parks across North America. The factory employed skilled carvers, painters, and engineers, blending artistry with industry. Today, the restored Herschell Carrousel Factory Museum preserves this unique legacy, allowing visitors to ride historic carousels and witness the craftsmanship that gave joy to generations.

MODERN IDENTITY

By the mid-20th century, the great lumber piles were gone, and heavy industry declined. Yet the Tonawandas adapted. Both cities turned toward their waterfronts, building marinas, bike trails, and parks. They also embraced heritage tourism, celebrating their industrial past while creating cultural and recreational amenities. Canal Fest of the Tonawandas, one of the largest canal-side festivals in New York, draws thousands each summer with music, parades, and fireworks, highlighting the enduring importance of the canal.

Today, the Tonawandas honor their Indigenous roots, canal-era prosperity, immigrant resilience, and industrial innovation. From the lively bars of Oliver Street to the artistry of Herschell's carousel horses, the twin cities continue to balance work, play, and history along the Niagara corridor.

Niagara Falls, USA

More than just a tourist attraction, Niagara Falls State Park embodies a vision of shared natural heritage.
Its creation set a precedent for conservation and public access that would inspire later movements, including
the establishment of the National Park System. To walk its paths is to experience not only the power of
water but also the enduring belief that such wonders belong to everyone.

Niagara Falls State Park is not only America's oldest state park—it is also one of its most awe-inspiring. Established in 1885 through the vision and persistence of landscape architect Frederick Law Olmsted and park advocate Thomas V. Welch, the park was created to protect the falls from unchecked industrial development. By the mid-19th century, mills, factories, and private enterprises had claimed much of the shoreline, charging admission for access and threatening to reduce the falls to a backdrop for industry. Olmsted and Welch believed that such a wonder of the natural world should not be commodified, but preserved as a place of beauty and inspiration open to all. Their advocacy led New York State to secure more than 400 acres of riverfront, creating a public sanctuary. Today, Niagara Falls State Park welcomes more than 9 million visitors each year and remains both a natural refuge and a cultural landmark.

Left to Right: The guided Niagara Falls Trolley gives passengers an overview of the State park. | Experience the underwater world at the Niagara Falls aquarium, boasting over 30 impressive exhibits and more than 200 aquatic animal species. | Niagara Falls are illuminated nightly with multi-colored LED lights starting at dusk | Great Lakes 360, the Aquarium's brand new expansion dedicated to the diverse ecosystems of the world's largest freshwater system.

THE FALLS EXPERIENCE

The park encompasses all three of Niagara's waterfalls–American Falls, Bridal Veil Falls, and Horseshoe Falls–each with its own character and drama. At Prospect Point, the entire span of the American Falls can be seen cascading into the gorge, framed by the skyline of Niagara Falls, New York. Just steps away, Luna Island offers an intimate perch between the Bridal Veil and American Falls, where the thunder of water surrounds visitors on both sides. Goat Island, the wooded centerpiece of the park, stretches deep into the river and provides unmatched perspectives. From Terrapin Point, visitors can gaze across the brink of Horseshoe Falls, where more than 600,000 gallons of water plunge every second. Few experiences in the world compare to standing so close to such immense natural power.

HISTORY AND CULTURAL LEGACY

Olmsted's design philosophy guided the creation of the park. He believed that natural scenery should be preserved with as little interference as

Left: Step onto the Cave of the Winds platforms and feel the full power of Niagara Falls–mist, roar, and rainbows all around you

Below: Generations of newlyweds begin their journey beside the thundering cascades.

possible. Instead of ornate gardens or artificial embellishments, the park was laid out with open lawns, shaded groves, and winding paths that framed the views rather than competing with them. That ethos remains visible today in the park's layout and vistas.

Beyond its natural setting, Niagara Falls also tells the story of human achievement. Monuments and plaques throughout the park commemorate innovators, explorers, and soldiers. One of the most notable figures is Nikola Tesla, whose groundbreaking work in hydroelectric power was first demonstrated at Niagara Falls in the 1890s. The success of Tesla's alternating current system helped electrify the modern world, making Niagara a birthplace of the global power industry.

ATTRACTIONS AND ACTIVITIES

The park offers far more than its scenic overlooks. The Maid of the Mist, in continuous operation since 1846, remains one of the most famous attractions in North America. Passengers don ponchos and board boats that travel directly into the basin of Horseshoe Falls, where the thunder, mist, and sheer scale of the cataract provide an unforgettable experience.

Another signature attraction is the Cave of the Winds. Visitors descend 175 feet into the gorge by elevator and step onto wooden walkways that bring them within feet of Bridal Veil Falls. Standing on the aptly named "Hurricane Deck," visitors are pounded by sheets of spray and wind as the falls crash beside them.

For those who prefer quiet adventure, the Niagara Gorge Trail System offers hiking routes that follow the river downstream. These trails range from easy walks through woodlands to more challenging scrambles along rocky cliffs, revealing the geology carved by the river over thousands of years.

SEASONS AND SCENERY

Every season transforms Niagara Falls State Park. In summer, crowds gather for boat tours, picnics, and outdoor events. Autumn brings brilliant foliage that frames the falls in fiery reds and golds. Winter is perhaps the most enchanting time: the mist freezes into towers of ice, the railings become frosted sculptures, and the falls roar through a world of crystalline silence. Spring adds another kind of drama as melting snow swells the river and new greenery brightens the park. Evening illuminations and seasonal fireworks make Niagara a spectacle year-round.

FROM HENNEPIN TO HONEYMOONS

The recorded history of Niagara Falls begins in 1678, when French priest and explorer Louis Hennepin published the first written description of the cataract. His account, declaring it "more prodigious than can be imagined," amazed European readers and fixed Niagara in the Western imagination.

By the early 19th century, improved transportation made the falls accessible to travelers, and it quickly became both a stage for daredevils and a place of romance. Tightrope walkers, barrel-riders, and stunt

performers risked their lives to thrill audiences. At the same time, the completion of the Erie Canal in 1825 opened the falls to a new audience–honeymooners. Thousands of newly married couples came to Niagara to begin their lives together, and the tradition was so enduring that the region earned its title as "the honeymoon capital of the world."

A TIMELESS LEGACY

Today, Niagara Falls State Park is more than a tourist attraction. It is the embodiment of a vision: that the greatest wonders of nature should be preserved for the enjoyment of all people. From roaring cataracts and wooded trails to monuments of invention and romance, the park is where nature, history, and human imagination converge. Nearly 140 years after its founding, Olmsted and Welch's dream still resonates–ensuring that Niagara Falls remains not just a destination, but a legacy shared by generations.

Above: Ride the Maid of the Mist and sail into the heart of Niagara Falls, surrounded by thunder, mist, and awe."

Opposite: Standing on Luna Island at the brink between the Bridal Veil and American Falls.

Niagara Falls, Ontario

Niagara Falls, Canada, is a world-famous destination with breathtaking waterfalls, exciting attractions, and stunning natural beauty. Whether you're looking for adventure or relaxation, you will find plenty to do in every season.

Niagara Falls, Ontario, is a city of contrasts–where the thundering Horseshoe Falls inspire awe, manicured gardens invite reflection, and neon lights beckon visitors toward carnival-like fun. It is both a natural wonder and a stage for spectacle, a place where stewardship and showmanship meet on the edge of the Niagara River.

At the heart of this balance is the Niagara Parks Commission, created in 1885 to preserve the river corridor while making it accessible to all. Today, its holdings stretch along the scenic Niagara Parkway, encompassing more than 1,300 hectares of green space. Queen Victoria Park, directly across from the Falls, sets the tone: formal flowerbeds, fragrant rose displays, and century-old shade trees soften the roar of cascading water.

Left to Right: Journey Behind the Falls, a unique view of the Falls from below and behind. | The Niagara SkyWheel gives riders a breathtaking panoramic view of the Falls. It towers 175 feet over the Niagara Falls horizon. | Eat a monsterous lunch on Clifton Hill | Be lunch at Dinosaur Adventure Golf

Seasonal plantings-vivid tulips in spring, chrysanthemums in autumn—ensure beauty year-round, while pathways invite leisurely strolls past fountains and overlooks.

Beyond the bustle of the central park, visitors discover the Niagara Parks Botanical Gardens, nearly 100 acres of themed landscapes nurtured by horticulture students. Its celebrated rose garden alone boasts more than 2,400 varieties. Next door, the Butterfly Conservatory adds a tropical flourish, where thousands of free-flying butterflies shimmer through a lush indoor rainforest. Further south, Dufferin Islands offer a quieter retreat: a chain of wooded islets threaded with bridges and home to waterfowl, songbirds, and reflective ponds.

Yet Niagara Falls is not solely about tranquility. Just steps from the parklands, Clifton Hill erupts in a blaze of lights, rides, arcades, and wax museums. Known as the "Street of Fun," it provides a carnival counterpoint to the majesty of the Falls. Families queue for Ferris wheels, haunted houses, and mini-golf under fluorescent skies, while restaurants and souvenir shops keep the energy humming late into the night.

As daylight fades, the natural and the theatrical converge. Powerful spotlights bathe the Falls in shifting colors, turning rushing water into a living canvas. Fireworks often crackle overhead, reflecting off the mist and the glass towers of nearby hotels. It is a nightly reminder that Niagara Falls, Ontario, thrives on dualities-wilderness and cultivation, serenity and spectacle. Visitors may come for the raw grandeur of the Horseshoe Falls, but they often linger in the city's gardens, parks, and playful attractions, where every side of Niagara's spirit is on display.

Opposite: The shaded lily ponds and formalized gardens offer visitors a tranquil escape in the heart of Niagara Falls

Right: Clifton Hill bursts with lights, games, and thrills on a carnival-style playground just steps from Niagara Falls.

Below: Soar above the Niagara Gorge on the Falls zipline—an unforgettable ride with a front-row view of nature's power.

Winter Festival of Lights

Each winter, Niagara Falls, Ontario, transforms into a glowing wonderland during the Winter Festival of Lights, a seasonal tradition that has become Canada's largest illumination festival. From mid-November through February, millions of lights, intricate displays, and dazzling projections brighten the long nights and cast the city in a festive glow.

The festival began in 1982 as a partnership between the Niagara Falls Canada Visitor Bureau and the Niagara Parks Commission. Originally conceived to extend the tourism season beyond summer, it has grown into a beloved celebration that now attracts more than a million visitors annually. Stretching along the Niagara Parkway, through Queen Victoria Park, Dufferin Islands, and into the city's tourist districts, the displays cover more than 8 kilometers of outdoor space.

Signature installations include the illuminated Canadian wildlife displays in Dufferin Islands, where deer, moose, and wolves crafted from thousands of tiny bulbs shimmer against snowy backdrops. Along the parkway, trees twinkle in rainbow hues, while the mighty Horseshoe Falls themselves become a canvas for ever-changing colors through powerful spotlights. More recent features, such as interactive light tunnels and digital projections on historic buildings, add modern flair to the festival's traditional charm.

Beyond the lights, the festival hosts concerts, fireworks, and cultural events, creating a multi-sensory experience. Families sip hot chocolate as they stroll among glowing arches; couples skate hand-in-hand at outdoor rinks; children marvel at lighted castles and animated displays.

The Winter Festival of Lights is more than decoration–it is a reminder that Niagara's magic doesn't fade with the end of summer. Against the icy mist of the Falls and the hush of snow-covered gardens, the festival transforms winter into a season of wonder, drawing visitors from near and far to celebrate light, community, and the enduring beauty of Niagara.

Lower River

The Lower Niagara River begins just below Niagara Falls, where the great cataract crashes over the escarpment and funnels into a narrow, turbulent gorge. For the next 14 miles, the river carves its way north to Lake Ontario, creating one of the most dramatic river landscapes in North America.

The first stretch below the falls is a study in raw power. Here the river becomes the Whirlpool Rapids, where churning whitewater races at nearly 30 miles per hour through a channel only a few hundred feet wide. The relentless force of this current makes it one of the most dangerous and awe-inspiring rapids in the world. A short distance downstream lies the Niagara Whirlpool, a massive natural basin formed thousands of years ago as the Falls eroded their way upriver. The swirling waters here, constantly changing with the flow, remain a favorite vantage point for visitors and scientists alike.

The gorge itself is a natural archive, its 300-foot cliffs revealing hundreds of millions of years of layered rock. Yet the Lower Niagara is not just about geology–it is also a corridor of history. Along its cliffs stands Devil's Hole, site of one of the bloodiest ambushes of the 18th century. In 1763, during Pontiac's Rebellion, Seneca warriors attacked a British supply train here, killing nearly every soldier and wagon driver in a fierce battle that echoed through the gorge. Half a century later, the War of 1812 again turned the Lower Niagara into a frontline, with battles at Queenston Heights and Lewiston shaping the border between nations.

Today, the Lower Niagara is protected as both natural wonder and recreational haven. Anglers line its banks for salmon and trout, hikers trace trails along the gorge rim, and boaters test its calmer waters near Lake Ontario. At the same time, its currents help fuel hydroelectric plants that power millions of homes.

In just 14 miles, the Lower Niagara compresses geology, ecology, and history into one of the most remarkable stretches of river anywhere in the world.

Opposite: From Queenston Heights, the Niagara River flows calm and wide. It's a peaceful contrast to the thunder of the Falls upstream.

NIAGARA UNIVERSITY

A Tradition of Education on the Gorge

Founded in 1856, Niagara University is a private Catholic institution perched on the U.S. side of the Niagara River gorge, just a few miles north of the Falls. Operated by the Vincentian Fathers, the university was established to provide higher education rooted in service, faith, and a commitment to community.

Originally called Our Lady of Angels Seminary, the school began with only a handful of students and faculty. Its early mission was to educate young men for the priesthood, but it quickly expanded to include broader liberal arts instruction. By the late 19th century, Niagara had grown into a recognized college, officially taking the name Niagara University in 1883.

The campus occupies a dramatic setting overlooking the Lower Niagara gorge, with views stretching toward Canada and Lake Ontario. Its location has long tied the school to the history and identity of the region. During the 20th century, Niagara expanded its offerings, establishing colleges of Business, Education, Nursing, and Hospitality, alongside strong programs in the liberal arts and sciences. The university also became known for its Division I athletics, particularly its storied basketball program, the Purple Eagles.

Today, Niagara University enrolls students from across the U.S. and abroad, while maintaining its Vincentian mission of service and social justice. Community outreach, international study, and local partnerships reflect its emphasis on learning with purpose. More than a campus on the gorge, Niagara University remains a cornerstone of education and cultural life in Western New York.

Opposite: Niagara University's campus overlooks the majestic Niagara River, blending academic tradition with breathtaking natural views.

Right: St. Vincent's Hall

Harnessing the Falls

For centuries, the thundering waters of Niagara Falls inspired awe, but in the late 19th century they also inspired a revolution. The Falls became one of the first places in the world where waterpower was transformed into large-scale electricity, forever changing both sides of the border.

EARLY INNOVATIONS

On the American side, experiments in hydropower began in the 1870s, when local mills used canal water to run machinery. In 1881, arc lights illuminated Niagara Falls for the first time using water-driven dynamos. But the breakthrough came in 1895 with the completion of the Niagara Falls Power Company's hydroelectric station. Designed with input from Nikola Tesla and George Westinghouse, it was the first plant to successfully transmit electricity over long distances using alternating current (AC). Power from the Falls flowed to Buffalo, 20 miles away, and eventually farther-an achievement that marked a turning point in the modern electrical age.

CANADIAN DEVELOPMENT

Canada pursued its own hydroelectric dream across the river. In 1922, Ontario Hydro (today Hydro One) completed the Sir Adam Beck Hydroelectric Generating Station. Named after the visionary politician who championed public power, the facility transformed southern Ontario's economy by supplying affordable electricity to homes, factories, and cities. The project was later expanded with the massive Sir Adam Beck II station and the Niagara River Control Works, which regulate water flow and storage through reservoirs. Together, these facilities can generate nearly 2,000 megawatts of electricity.

MODERN POWERHOUSES

On the U.S. side, the Robert Moses Niagara Power Plant opened in 1961 after a devastating rockslide destroyed earlier facilities. With its 13 turbines, it remains New York State's largest hydropower station, capable of producing more than 2,500 megawatts. Along with the adjacent Lewiston Pump Generating Plant, it provides reliable renewable energy to millions of homes and businesses.

Today, the hydropower plants at Niagara represent one of the world's largest binational renewable energy systems. They embody a balance between spectacle and utility, ensuring that Niagara Falls remains both a global icon and a working engine of clean energy.

The Robert Moses Niagara Power Plant showcases the might of the river, transforming the force of Niagara Falls into clean, renewable hydroelectric power.

Freedom Crossing

The Underground Railroad Along the Niagara River

The Niagara River's role in the Underground Railroad underscores its dual identity: a formidable natural barrier and a symbol of deliverance. Along its banks, geography and humanity intersected, making the river not only a wonder of nature but also a lifeline to liberty.

THE RIVER AS BARRIER AND GATEWAY

The Niagara River, narrow but swift, was both a peril and a promise. For enslaved men, women, and children fleeing bondage, these turbulent waters marked the final barrier separating the United States from Canada. On the far shore lay freedom, secured when Britain abolished slavery in 1834. The roar of the Falls and the sweep of the river reminded fugitives of the dangers still ahead–but also of the liberty waiting just across the current.

CROSSING POINTS TO FREEDOM

Several routes along the river became legendary. In Buffalo, Broderick Park served as a lifeline. Here, freedom seekers boarded ferries or small boats bound for Fort Erie, aided by sympathetic ferrymen and local activists. Farther downstream, Lewiston offered another dramatic crossing. Abolitionist Josiah Tryon, a humble tailor and church deacon, became known as Lewiston's "station master." By night, he guided fugitives down perilous paths carved into the gorge, leading them to waiting rowboats that carried them across to Queenston. Oral histories recall Tryon's quiet, steadfast courage–his small acts of kindness multiplied into countless journeys to freedom.

At Niagara Falls, the completion of the Suspension Bridge in 1855 offered yet another path. Stretching high above the gorge, it provided fugitives a daring but discreet way into Canada. Hidden among crowds of travelers or escorted by allies, freedom seekers crossed on foot or by train over the bridge, the roar of the cataracts echoing below. One of the most powerful

Opposite: The "Freedom Crossing" monument in Lewiston by Susan Geissler depicts a slave mother, father, and child ready to be taken across the river in a rowboat by Tryon, a volunteer "station master."

exhibits at today's Niagara Falls Underground Railroad Heritage Center recreates this crossing, reminding visitors of the peril and exhilaration felt by those who walked it.

TUBMAN'S PRESENCE IN THE REGION

Harriet Tubman herself–already legendary as "Moses" of the Underground Railroad–was active in Western New York. She personally escorted groups of fugitives to the river and across into Canada, and she drew upon the strong abolitionist networks in Buffalo, Niagara Falls, and Rochester. Tubman's presence underscored the importance of this borderland: Niagara was not just another stop, but one of the most decisive gateways on the road to freedom.

PRESERVING THE STORY

Today, the Niagara River corridor is rich with memorials to this hidden history. Broderick Park commemorates the Buffalo crossing, Lewiston honors

Right: The Michigan Street Baptist Church, erected in 1845, was a legendary Underground Railroad station. The building provided refuge for hundreds of freedom seekers before they crossed the border to Canada.

Later the church became a meeting place for abolitionists and anti-lynching activists like Frederick Douglass, William Wells Brown, W.E.B. Du Bois, and Booker T. Washington, each of whom graced its sanctuary. The Michigan Street Baptist Church has been a central part of the history and culture of the African-American community in Buffalo for more than 170 years.

Josiah Tryon with plaques and heritage programming, and the Underground Railroad Heritage Center in Niagara Falls immerses visitors in the human stories of courage and solidarity. Together, these sites reveal the density of Underground Railroad activity in a single river corridor, unmatched anywhere else in North America.also a lifeline to liberty.

Above: In the 1850s, Harriet Tubman led groups of freedom seekers across the Niagara Suspension Bridge, a daring new crossing high above the gorge. Hidden among travelers or moving under cover of night, they passed from the United States into Canada, beyond the reach of slave catchers. For many, this bridge marked the final, breathtaking step on the long road to freedom.

This bridge was dismantled in 1897 after serving for nearly 40 years. It was replaced by the Whirlpool bridge.

Niagara Parkway

he Niagara Parkway is more than a road–it is a living museum and garden, managed by the Niagara Parks Commission. Its scenic bike path is one of Canada's longest recreational trails, and its viewpoints draw millions of visitors annually. In the words of Winston Churchill, who once toured it in 1943, the Niagara Parkway is "the prettiest Sunday afternoon drive in the world.

CANADA'S MOST SCENIC DRIVE

Few roadways in North America can rival the Niagara Parkway for beauty and historical significance. Hugging the Canadian side of the Niagara River for nearly 35 miles (56 kilometers), the parkway stretches from Fort Erie in the south to Niagara-on-the-Lake in the north, offering motorists, cyclists, and walkers a continuous ribbon of scenery, heritage, and recreation.

ORIGINS AND DESIGN

The idea for the parkway originated in the early 20th century, when conservationists and planners envisioned a landscaped route that would connect the natural wonder of Niagara Falls with the broader cultural landscape of the Niagara Peninsula. Officially opened in 1931, the roadway was designed as more than just a transportation corridor. It was conceived as a linear park, lined with picnic areas, walking paths, gardens, and historical markers that invite visitors to pause and reflect.

Left to Right: The Niagara Butterfly Conservatory houses over 2,000 vibrant butterflies flutter freely among tropical flowers and winding paths. | Whirlpool Aero Car | Niagara Botanical Gardens, a 99-acre oasis of vibrant blooms, peaceful pathways, and seasonal beauty. | The historic McFarland Tea House in Niagara-on-the-Lake offers timeless charm in the elegance of a 19th-century home meets the comfort of a classic tearoom.

HIGHLIGHTS ALONG THE PARKWAY

The parkway's most famous section passes directly alongside the thundering Horseshoe Falls, offering one of the most dramatic roadside views in the world. Yet the drive reveals far more than the falls themselves. Just north lies the Niagara Parks Botanical Gardens, a 99-acre landscape of themed gardens and arboretums, home to nearly 2,400 roses in peak bloom. Nestled within the gardens is the Butterfly Conservatory, where thousands of tropical butterflies drift among lush plantings and waterfalls, delighting visitors year-round.

Further along, travelers encounter whimsical landmarks such as the Floral Clock, a massive working timepiece planted with colorful seasonal flowers. Nearby, the Whirlpool Aero Car, suspended by sturdy cables, carries passengers high above the swirling waters of the Niagara Whirlpool, offering a thrilling aerial perspective of the gorge.

At Queenston Heights, history takes center stage. The site of a decisive War of 1812 battle, it is crowned by Brock's Monument, a towering column that honors Major General Sir Isaac Brock, the British commander who fell in the battle. From here, panoramic views stretch across the river into New York State.

JOURNEY'S END

South of the falls, the parkway winds toward Fort Erie, tracing the river's calmer reaches. Historic Old Fort Erie recalls another chapter of the War of 1812, while quiet pull-offs invite travelers to watch sailboats, migrating birds, or even ice floes in winter. To the north, the road culminates in the orchards, vineyards, and 19th-century streetscapes of Niagara-on-the-Lake, Canada's most charming small town.

Left: Brock's Monument is a 185 ft column atop Queenston Heights dedicated to Major General Sir Isaac Brock, one of Canada's heroes of the War of 1812. Brock, a British Army officer in charge of defending Upper Canada from a United States invasion.

Opposite: The Floral Clock on the Niagara Parkway is a living timepiece, crafted from thousands of colorful flowers arranged in intricate patterns that change with the seasons. A beloved roadside landmark since 1950, it combines horticultural artistry with precise mechanics, delighting visitors with both beauty and accuracy.

A Strong Cultural Current

The Niagara River is a natural wonder, but it is equally a cultural corridor. It guides visitors not only through landscapes of rock and water but through galleries, theaters, historic homes, and performance spaces. By clustering so many cultural assets along its banks, the river underscores a truth: culture, like water, flows best when it moves, connects, and inspires. To travel the Niagara is to travel a living current of arts, history, and entertainment—one that carries forward the shared identity of a region shaped by both nature and creativity.

A Corridor of Arts, History, & Entertainment

The Niagara River is often celebrated for its thundering falls and dramatic gorge, but just as powerful is the cultural current that flows along its 36 miles. From the shores of Lake Erie to the mouth of Lake Ontario, the river stitches together a constellation of museums, theaters, historic homes, and performance spaces. This corridor of culture transforms the river into more than a natural wonder—it becomes a stage, a gallery, and a classroom, offering a journey where art and history flow seamlessly with the water.

Art on the Banks

At the river's southern end, where it spills out of Lake Erie, Buffalo anchors the cultural landscape. Among its many institutions, the Castellani Art Museum at Niagara University stands out as a beacon for the visual arts directly overlooking the Niagara Gorge. Founded by philanthropists Armand and Eleanor Castellani, the museum holds a collection of more than 5,000 works, ranging from contemporary American art to pieces by European masters. Its exhibitions and educational programs make it a crossroads of creativity, situating global conversations about art within the unique setting of the Niagara River.

The Castellani reflects a broader truth about the river corridor: cultural institutions here are rarely divorced from their geography. The roar of the falls and the drama of the gorge imbue the museum with a sense of place, making the experience of art inseparable from the surrounding landscape.

Lewiston: Artpark and the Living Landscape

A few miles downstream, the village of Lewiston transforms the cliffs of the gorge into a vast outdoor cultural campus at Artpark. Established in 1974 on the site of an abandoned industrial zone, Artpark demonstrates the regenerative power of culture. Its amphitheater, outdoor sculpture gardens, and artist residencies have hosted performances ranging from symphony

Opposite: Castellani Art Museum at Niagara University

RiverBrink

concerts and Broadway musicals to rock legends and avant-garde theater. Sculptural installations dot the parkland, allowing visitors to encounter creativity against the backdrop of the river's wild beauty.

Artpark epitomizes the Niagara River as a cultural artery–its programming merges landscape, performance, and community engagement. By situating art within nature, it continues a regional tradition of seeing the river not only as scenery but as inspiration and collaborator.

NIAGARA-ON-THE-LAKE: THEATER AND HERITAGE

Crossing to the Canadian side, the river's cultural current carries visitors into Niagara-on-the-Lake, a town that pairs historic preservation with world-class theater. At its heart is the Shaw Festival, founded in 1962 and now one of North America's leading repertory companies. Each season, its stages host a mix of plays by George Bernard Shaw, his contemporaries, and modern playwrights, drawing audiences from around the globe. The festival transforms the town into a cultural destination where theatergoers spill out into historic streetscapes, linking performance with place.

Nearby, the McFarland House, built in 1800 and preserved by the Niagara Parks Commission, offers a different dimension of cultural heritage. As one of the oldest homes in the region, it connects visitors to the early Loyalist settlers who shaped the Niagara frontier. The house has served as an inn, a military hospital during the War of 1812, and now as a museum, offering tea service in its historic conservatory. Standing just above the river, it is a reminder that history along the Niagara is not confined to battlefields and forts but is also written in the domestic lives of its people.

QUEENSTON: RIVERBRINK ART MUSEUM

Continuing north, the river narrows at Queenston, where the RiverBrink Art Museum overlooks its waters. Housed in the former country estate of Samuel Weir, a Canadian lawyer and art collector, RiverBrink showcases a collection of Canadian, European, and Indigenous art. The galleries emphasize Canada's cultural heritage, with works by members of the Group of Seven, Cornelius Krieghoff, and Emily Carr. Its location, perched above the river, reinforces the connection between landscape and artistic vision, framing the Niagara not just as a subject of art but as a setting for cultural preservation.

RiverBrink also plays a role in linking Canadian identity with the shared cross-border heritage of the Niagara. Exhibits often highlight how the river has inspired painters and writers on both sides, making it a symbol of cultural unity as much as a geographic divide.

LAKE ONTARIO AND THE WIDER WORLD

As the Niagara River empties into Lake Ontario, its cultural journey broadens. The river has carried not only water but also ideas, traditions, and performances, drawing people from across the world to its banks. From the Castellani's modern galleries to Artpark's amphitheater, from the Shaw Festival's stages to RiverBrink's historic estate, the corridor presents a continuous sequence of cultural experiences. The McFarland House completes the picture, grounding the artistic in the historical and reminding visitors that culture is both lived and performed.

The clustering of these institutions along the river is no coincidence. Each site capitalizes on the power of place–the inspiration of water, the drama of the gorge, the symbolism of borders and crossings. Together, they form a necklace of cultural gems, strung along a river that connects more than lakes. It connects communities, histories, and imaginations.

Right: A bronze statue of Nobel Prize–winning playwright George Bernard Shaw honors the inspiration behind Niagara-on-the-Lake's world-renowned Shaw Festival, celebrating theater, wit, and cultural legacy. Since 1962, The Shaw Festival Theatre has lit up the stage with world-class performances.

Lewiston, New York

Lewiston's story is one of continuity: from Indigenous portage trail to battlefield, from frontier outpost to vibrant village. Its riverside setting continues to connect people across borders, just as it has for centuries.

PORTAGE, BATTLEFIELD, AND CULTURAL VILLAGE

Lewiston, New York, rests at a bend in the Niagara River just below the escarpment, a location that shaped its destiny for centuries. Long before Europeans arrived, the Haudenosaunee used Lewiston as the southern end of the portage route around Niagara Falls. Canoes and trade goods were carried along this trail to Lake Ontario, making it a crossroads of cultures and commerce.

The French and later the British recognized this importance, fortifying the Lower Niagara and linking Lewiston to their colonial ambitions. After the American Revolution, settlers arrived, drawn by fertile farmland and trade opportunities. John Lewiston, for whom the village is named, laid out the town in the early 19th century, and taverns, stores, and warehouses soon lined its streets.

Lewiston's most dramatic moment came during the War of 1812. On October 13, 1812, American forces crossed the river to seize Queenston Heights. They briefly captured the high ground but were driven back by British reinforcements and Haudenosaunee allies. The battle cost the life of British

Left to Right: Frontier House in Lewiston, NY, stands as a grand reminder of early American hospitality-an 1824 stone inn that once welcomed presidents, pioneers, and travelers along the Niagara frontier. | The Whirlpool Jet Boats roar through the Niagara River's rapids, offering an adrenaline-filled ride through towering waves and breathtaking gorge scenery. | Set into the Niagara River gorge, the Artpark amphitheater blends nature and performance. | Silo Restaurant - taste history and enjoy the river view while dining in a converted coal silo!

General Isaac Brock, now remembered as a Canadian hero. A year later, in December 1813, Lewiston was burned to the ground during the British counteroffensive, forcing residents to rebuild from ruins.

Through the 19th century, Lewiston thrived as a river town. Steamboats docked here, carrying passengers and goods, even after the Erie Canal shifted regional trade. The community became known for its wharves, churches, and schools, and later for its role in the Underground Railroad.

Today, Lewiston honors its past while embracing the arts. The historic Frontier House still anchors downtown, while Artpark, a performance venue carved into the river cliffs, hosts concerts, theater, and festivals each summer. Together, history and creativity make Lewiston one of the Niagara Frontier's most distinctive villages.

Opposite: The Lewiston Opera Hall, built in the 19th century, served as a vibrant cultural hub where townspeople gathered for plays, concerts, lectures, and community events. Its stage brought world-class entertainment to a small village, leaving behind a legacy of music, drama, and shared experiences that helped shape Lewiston's cultural identity.

Above: Reenactors bring the Battle of Queenston Heights to life, honoring history with muskets, uniforms, and timeless courage.

Niagara Wine Country:
A Binational Toast

Few river corridors in North America offer such a distinctive wine landscape as the Niagara region, straddling both the United States and Canada. On either shore of the lower Niagara River, fertile soils, lake-moderated climates, and centuries of agricultural tradition have combined to create a thriving cross-border wine country that attracts connoisseurs and casual tasters alike.
Together, these two wine regions showcase how geography unites rather than divides.

ONTARIO'S NIAGARA PENINSULA

On the Canadian side, the Niagara Peninsula has earned international acclaim. More than 100 wineries spread across sub-appellations like Niagara-on-the-Lake, the Beamsville Bench, and the Twenty Valley. The region's unique microclimate—created by the shelter of the Niagara Escarpment and the tempering effect of Lake Ontario—allows for the cultivation of cool-climate varietals such as Riesling, Chardonnay, and Pinot Noir. Most famously, Ontario is celebrated as the world's leading producer of Icewine, a sweet, concentrated nectar made from grapes harvested and pressed while naturally frozen on the vine. Visitors weave between vineyards and villages, enjoying not just wine tastings but also fine dining, festivals, and sweeping views of orchards and lakefront landscapes.

NEW YORK'S NIAGARA WINE TRAIL

On the American side, the Niagara Wine Trail anchors itself in Niagara and Orleans counties. Here, family-run wineries flourish along country roads north of Buffalo, extending eastward toward Rochester. The proximity to Lake Ontario also plays a vital role in moderating temperatures, protecting vines from winterkill, and extending the growing season. American wineries emphasize a mix of vinifera grapes—Cabernet Franc, Chardonnay, and Riesling—alongside hybrids like Vidal Blanc and native varieties such as Concord and Niagara. The result is a broad palette of wines that range from crisp and dry to sweet and fruit-forward, reflecting the diversity of the region's agricultural heritage. The U.S. trail offers a relaxed, small-farm charm that pairs well with local cheese, produce, and agritourism experiences.

Niagara Parks

For nearly 140 years, Niagara Parks has ensured that the natural spectacle of the Falls is complemented by cultural, historical, and recreational experiences. By blending gardens with battlegrounds, and scenic overlooks with restored heritage sites, the Commission has transformed the Niagara River into a corridor of living history and environmental beauty. It remains a model of how a single agency can protect a natural wonder while also enriching it with art, heritage, and entertainment for generations of visitors.

PRESERVING A RIVER OF BEAUTY AND HERITAGE

The Niagara Parks Commission–commonly known simply as Niagara Parks–has been a guardian of the Niagara River corridor for well over a century. Established in 1885, this Ontario agency was created to preserve and enhance the natural beauty of Niagara Falls while also protecting the broader shoreline of the Niagara River as public greenspace.

Its mandate balances conservation with accessibility, ensuring that millions of annual visitors can enjoy both the majesty of the Falls and the cultural landmarks woven into the landscape.

A CORRIDOR OF PARKS AND TRAILS

Today, Niagara Parks manages more than 6 square miles of parkland stretching along the Canadian side of the river,

Niagara Glen

McFarland House

Chippawa Battlefield Park

Queen Victoria Park

anchored by the Niagara Parkway, a 36-mile scenic road running from Fort Erie to Niagara-on-the-Lake. Within this corridor, the Commission oversees trails, gardens, picnic grounds, historic homes, and interpretive centers. Over time, it has experimented with various ways to manage the crush of tourists, including operating a shuttle bus system called the People Mover to reduce automobile congestion near the Falls. Niagara Parks once even managed Navy Island under a lease agreement with Parks Canada, showing how its role extended beyond simple landscaping to stewardship of nationally significant heritage sites.

CULTURAL AND NATURAL ATTRACTIONS

The attractions under Niagara Parks' umbrella represent a wide range of history, entertainment, and environmental education. Together, they showcase why the Niagara River is more than just a natural wonder–it is also a cultural corridor.

• **Chippawa Battlefield Park** commemorates a key War of 1812 clash.

• **Old Fort Erie**, another War of 1812 landmark, is preserved as a National Historic Site.

• **Laura Secord Homestead**, the home of Canada's famous heroine, tells the story of her courageous 1813 walk to warn British forces.

• **McFarland House**, dating to 1800, offers a glimpse into Loyalist domestic life.

• **Mackenzie Printery** preserves the presses once used by William Lyon Mackenzie, an influential journalist and political leader.

The Commission also maintains vibrant landscapes: Dufferin Islands, a cluster of secluded islands perfect for quiet exploration; Queen Victoria Park, a manicured centerpiece in the heart of Niagara Falls; and the Niagara Glen Nature Reserve, where trails wind down into the gorge to reveal ancient geology and rare plant life.

Horticulture is central to Niagara Parks' identity. The Niagara Parks

School of Horticulture trains gardeners and landscape designers, while the adjacent Botanical Gardens and Butterfly Conservatory delight the public with colorful seasonal displays and tropical butterfly species. The Floral Showhouse and the iconic Floral Clock continue the tradition of horticultural artistry, linking gardening to civic pride.

SCENIC RIDES AND VISITOR EXPERIENCES

Many of the most memorable experiences in Niagara come through attractions run by Niagara Parks. The Whirlpool Aero Car, designed in 1916, still carries visitors high above the swirling whirlpool of the Lower Niagara. The White Water Walk brings them close to Class VI rapids along a quarter-mile boardwalk. At the Falls themselves, the Table Rock Welcome Centre offers shops, restaurants, and observation decks, along with the dramatic Journey Behind the Falls, a series of tunnels leading to platforms just steps away from Horseshoe Falls' curtain of water. Nearby, the Falls Incline Railway connects the Table Rock area with the hotels on the Fallsview ridge, while Hornblower Niagara Cruises (formerly Maid of the Mist) provides the classic boat ride into the mist of the Falls. The recently restored Niagara Parks Power Station, a century-old hydroelectric plant, now interprets the engineering marvels that first harnessed the river's energy, combining artifact displays with interactive storytelling.

THE NIAGARA HERITAGE TRAIL

Perhaps the most ambitious project completed by the Commission is the Niagara Heritage Trail, a scenic and historic pathway that runs the entire 35-mile Canadian shoreline of the river from Fort Erie to Niagara-on-the-Lake. Planned in the 1980s and completed in 1995, the trail passes by many of the Commission's crown jewels, including the Butterfly Conservatory, the Botanical Gardens, and the Whirlpool Golf Course. At its center is Queen Victoria Park, where floral displays, concerts, and seasonal festivals anchor the tourist experience.

Opposite: Stroll the Niagara River Walk and enjoy serene paths, rushing waters, and breathtaking views along the gorge.
Right: At the Niagara Falls Floral Showcase, vibrant blooms and exotic plants create a garden paradise year-round.

Youngstown, New York

The War of 1812 is a poignant reminder that war can happen as close as your backyard. Much of that fighting occurred right along the U.S. and Canadian border.

A FRONTIER VILLAGE AT THE RIVER'S MOUTH

At the northern tip of the Niagara River, where its swift waters empty into Lake Ontario, sits Youngstown, New York–a small village with a history that belies its quiet appearance. This is one of the most strategic and storied places on the Niagara frontier, a crossroads where Indigenous heritage, colonial ambition, and the struggle for nationhood all intersected.

INDIGENOUS AND COLONIAL ROOTS

For centuries before Europeans arrived, the Lower Niagara was a homeland for the Haudenosaunee, especially the Seneca Nation. The river's mouth served as both a natural highway and a fortified boundary. Control of this narrow but vital waterway meant influence over trade and travel between the Great Lakes and the Atlantic. Recognizing its importance, the French built Fort Niagara here in 1726, followed by expansions that made it one of the strongest posts in New France. The British seized the fort during the French and Indian War in 1759, a turning point that shifted power in the Great Lakes.

Opposite: Guarding the mouth of the Niagara River for over 300 years, Old Fort Niagara showcases French, British, and American history through stone bastions, living history programs, and sweeping views of Lake Ontario.

Left to Right: Boats at the Youngstown Yacht Club | Fort Niagara Light, an historic lighthouse overlooking the Niagara River's gateway. | Aerial view of Youngstown's business district | Quaint Youngstown shops

BIRTH OF A VILLAGE

The civilian settlement that grew near the fort became the nucleus of Youngstown. After the American Revolution, settlers were drawn by fertile farmland and opportunities created by the garrison. John Young, one of the area's early developers, lent his name to the village when he formally laid out plots in the early 1800s.

THE WAR OF 1812

Youngstown's most turbulent chapter came during the War of 1812. The village sat squarely in the line of fire between American and British forces. In May 1813, American troops crossed the river to capture Fort George, directly opposite Youngstown in Niagara-on-the-Lake. But the tide turned that December, when British and Indigenous forces struck back, crossing into Youngstown, burning the village, and advancing south to destroy Lewiston and beyond. Like many frontier communities, Youngstown was reduced to ashes, only to be painstakingly rebuilt by determined residents.

LIFE AFTER WAR

During the 19th century, Youngstown developed into a modest port and farming hub. Fishing fleets launched from its shoreline into Lake Ontario, while its docks handled lumber, grain, and produce. Though the opening of the Erie Canal in 1825 shifted major trade toward Buffalo, Youngstown maintained local importance as a river community and remained linked to the rhythms of Fort Niagara, which continued as an active military post.

A LIVING HERITAGE

Today, Youngstown retains the atmosphere of a village steeped in history. Its streets still echo with 19th-century architecture, and its riverfront parks offer sweeping views across to Canada. The village is inseparable from Old Fort Niagara, now a world-class historic site and museum that draws visitors from across the globe.

Niagara-on-the-Lake, Ontario

Nestled at the mouth of the Niagara River where it meets Lake Ontario, Niagara-on-the-Lake is often called Canada's most picturesque small town. But beyond its tree-lined streets, vineyards, and historic storefronts lies a remarkable story that blends Indigenous heritage, Loyalist settlement, war, and cultural rebirth.

NIAGARA-ON-THE-LAKE: CANADA'S FIRST CAPITAL

Originally a Seneca and later Mississauga settlement, the area became strategically important during the late 18th century, when British Loyalists fleeing the American Revolution sought refuge in Upper Canada. In 1781, a small community formed on the river's west bank, known first as Butlersburg and later as Newark.

By 1792, Newark was chosen as the first capital of Upper Canada. Governor John Graves Simcoe directed its early civic planning, even envisioning a network of roads that would eventually shape southern Ontario.

The town's prominence was short-lived. In 1796, the capital moved to York (Toronto) for security reasons, but Niagara remained a vital military and commercial hub. During the War

Left to Right: From classic comedies to bold new works, the Shaw Festival offers an unforgettable theater experience in the scenic beauty of Niagara-on-the-Lake. he Shaw Festival in Niagara-on-the-Lake brings George Bernard Shaw and contemporary playwrights to life on stage, | Step inside Canada's first licensed pharmacy, circa 1869. | Niagara-on-the-Lake Visitors Center/Chamber Of Commerce and the Clock Tower: the heart of Queen Street's charm. | Step back into the War of 1812 at Fort George in Niagara-on-the-Lake, where costumed interpreters, musket demonstrations, and historic ramparts bring Canada's early military past vividly to life.

of 1812, its location on the American border made it a target. U.S. forces occupied and later burned the town in December 1813, leaving it in ruins. Residents slowly rebuilt, and the reconstructed Georgian-style homes and public buildings that line Queen Street today reflect this post-war determination.

Throughout the 19th century, Niagara-on-the-Lake thrived as a port, a shipbuilding center, and eventually a resort destination. Steamships carried tourists from Toronto across Lake Ontario, and wealthy families established summer residences. By the 20th century, its charm and heritage made it a natural stage for the Shaw Festival, founded in 1962, which has since grown into one of North America's premier repertory theater companies.

Today, Niagara-on-the-Lake is celebrated not only for its theater but also for its wineries, gardens, and well-preserved streetscapes. Designated a National Historic District, it embodies a rare balance: a living town that honors its Loyalist roots, remembers its wartime scars, and flourishes as a cultural beacon on the Niagara frontier.

Niagara-on-the-Lake blooms with charm with streets lined with vibrant flowers that make the whole town feel like a garden

It's Been An Amazing Journey

The Niagara River's path embodies both tranquility and significance.
It is a place where history, ecology, and geography converge,
a reminder that even the world's most dramatic rivers ultimately find calm
as they finish their course.

After a turbulent 36-mile passage from Lake Erie, the Niagara River completes its journey as it empties into Lake Ontario. This final stretch is less dramatic than the thunderous Falls or the roaring Whirlpool Rapids, but no less significant. Here, the river widens, slows, and takes on a sense of completion, carrying the waters of the upper Great Lakes one step closer to the Atlantic Ocean.

North of Lewiston, New York, and Queenston, Ontario, the gorge opens, and the Lower Niagara broadens into a calmer channel. The riverbanks host two historic communities—Youngstown on the American side and Niagara-on-the-Lake on the Canadian side. For centuries, this confluence has been a place of trade, settlement, and conflict. Indigenous peoples, French explorers, British soldiers, and American settlers all recognized the strategic importance of this meeting of river and lake. Fort Niagara, still standing guard at the river's mouth, is a powerful reminder of this layered past.

As the river merges with Lake Ontario, it completes a journey that began far to the west, with waters flowing from Lake Superior, Michigan, and Huron through Erie, down the Niagara, and onward to Ontario. From there, the current continues through the St. Lawrence River to the Atlantic.

Opposite: The Niagara River as it passes past Old Fort Niagara out to Lake Ontario

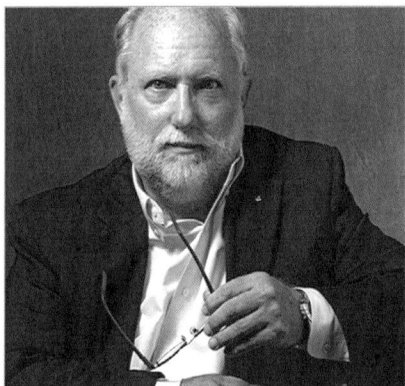

Mark Donnelly, PhD. – Author & Photographer

Mark Donnelly, PhD., is an accomplished author, artist, and educator whose life and work are deeply rooted in Western New York. A passionate advocate for the region's waterfront, he brings history, culture, and community together through both words and images. Beyond his former professional accomplishments as a college professor, branding consultant, and newspaper publisher, he is a proud husband, father of four remarkable adult children, a committed Mason, and, true to form, rarely without his camera in hand.

The author of over 50 published books, Dr. Donnelly has chronicled the spirit and resilience of Buffalo and the Niagara Frontier in works such as The Fine Art of Capturing Buffalo, Frozen Assets, Statuesque Buffalo, There's So Much To Love, Shovel Ready City, Celebrating Buffalo's Waterfront, and A City Built by Giants. His creativity also extends to children's literature and whimsical novelty cookbooks, reflecting his wide-ranging curiosity and sense of play.

An award-winning photographer, his images have been featured in regional and national exhibitions, with showings at the Albright-Knox Art Gallery, Burchfield Penney Art Center, Rodman Arts Centre, CEPA Gallery, The NACC, Big Orbit Gallery, Seattle Art Museum, ZGM Gallery, and the Art Gallery of Hamilton. Whether through prose or photography, Dr. Donnelly continues to celebrate the stories, landscapes, and communities that make Western New York unique.

Portrait by David Moog

www.ingramcontent.com/pod-product-compliance
Lightning Source LLC
Chambersburg PA
CBRC100752100426
42812CB00023B/2670